50 DRAMATIC

50 Dramatic Monologues

DAVID BURT

ISBN 1 84291 170 8

Published by
KINGSWAY COMMUNICATIONS LTD
Lottbridge Drove, Eastbourne BN23 6NT, England.
Email: books@kingsway.co.uk

Book design and production for the publishers by
Bookprint Creative Services, P.O. Box 827, BN21 3YJ, England.
Printed in Great Britain.

For my 100% perfect girl

Contents

Acknowledgements

Before we start, I would like to doff my hat to the veritable feast of people that have been behind this project.

To all those who have had moments of inspiration and suggested different characters for inclusion in the collection, I give thanks. To all those who have performed or listened to early drafts of the scripts, I also thank them for their participation and patience.

And, above all, I thank my amazing family and friends for their continued support and for tolerating my ever-increasing eccentricities.

Finally, thanks to all of you who use your time, talent and energy to perform – without you, this has truly been a waste of time!

Introduction

The curtain opens on an empty stage. There is no set or props visible, and a single spotlight illuminates the centre of the desolate platform. The audience fall silent as a solitary performer steps slowly into the circle of light and, with head raised, begins to speak . . .

The power of the monologue

I must confess I've always had a particular liking for a good monologue. Of course I also enjoy a well-performed sketch or play, but there's something rather special about the mono-logue form – one person in front of an audience, creating a situation, character and atmosphere all on their own.

Part of my love of the monologue has come from seeing some of our best actors performing different pieces over the years – Steven Berkoff, Tom Courtenay, Patrick Stewart, Ian Richardson and Maggie Smith, to name a few. Something very special is created when the limitation of one performer on stage causes an audience to do some work of their own and engage their imaginations.

As a performer, I've also particularly enjoyed practising the art of the monologue. Once you get past the initial nervous feeling of being out there on your own, it can provide the closest form of communication with an audience. But, before I start to sound overly artsy, I think the real power of the monologue is in its incredible simplicity. Although learning the lines can be a bit of a pain (more on this later), a monologue performed well should always prove to be a real crowd-pleaser. More than any other dramatic art form, the monologue provides us with the opportunity of really getting to know a character better.

Peeling back the layers

In a sketch or play, it can sometimes be difficult to understand exactly what a character is feeling. Of course, if it is well written and acted, we should have a fairly clear picture, but because we only hear what the character says, we might not know what he thinks or exactly how he feels. Yes, we can read between the lines, but we have to work to get there.

The exception to this rule is 'dramatic asides'. Think of some of Shakespeare's characters, breaking out of a scene to tell the audience their innermost thoughts. The monologue format allows us to do this all the time. As the character speaks directly to the audience, it is in effect a confessional. They can narrate a story, describe events, recall dialogue, but most importantly they can say openly what they think.

I've split this collection into six different sections, so hopefully there should be something to suit most situations.

1. Easter. I originally wrote most pieces in this section for a project I was working on in a local secondary school. I've chosen a wide range of characters, and each gives their account of events leading up to, during and after Christ's crucifixion. Although the pieces provide some laughs, on the whole I hope they are moving or challenging in content. They are ideal for use either on their own or grouped together with some music for a longer Easter presentation.

2. Christmas. I've used a mixture of serious and slightly sillier pieces here, to suit your occasion. The wonderful array of colourful characters and strange happenings described in the gospel accounts of Christ's birth allows for an interesting range of monologues – a talking donkey and harassed innkeeper's wife, to name but two!

3. Seven Ages of Man.   This section again can be performed separately or as a larger, linked presentation. Taking the wider themes of 'What's the meaning of life?' and 'Where are we going?', the collection opens up seven windows on the life of a character called Vince, ranging from his birth to extreme old age.

4. Bible Characters.   On the whole I've opted for reasonably well-known characters in this section. The joy of writing biblical monologues is the huge choice of possible material. When choosing a character, you can use the monologue form either to introduce a lesser known person, teaching the listener about the part they play, or to present a well-loved character, having fun allowing them to make comment on known events.

5. Bible Observers.   I think I had the most fun writing this section, really exploiting the full use of the monologue's power. Instead of telling a story through the eyes of the main character, I've written from the new perspective of a fictionalised observer. Beware, some of these are ever so slightly daft! Imagine the story of the miraculous catch of fish from a guppy's view! (I warned you.)

6. Contemporary.   As well as using monologues to tell Bible stories, we can create contemporary characters to help explain morals or Christian truth. The best way to work these is to decide on a topic you wish to explore, then create a character to illustrate this view. I've looked at subjects varying from debt and anorexia to survival of the fittest and the kingdom of God.

So, that's what you've got coming at you over the course of the next few hundred pages. I think there should be something suitable for everyone. I hope I haven't made the monologue seem too daunting. Certainly from a performance point of view it is not the easiest thing in the world to do well, but by putting some work in, the final outcome is well worth it. Apart from feeling a bit isolated on stage, what puts most people off before they even start is the terrible thought of learning the words! That leads me nicely on to the next section . . .

To learn or not to learn

'I'd love to do a monologue but there's no way I could learn all the words!' This is a familiar cry when people consider performing a monologue, but fear not! I have a couple of answers. First – if you really want to, and are willing to put your mind to it, I really believe you can learn the monologue, and I've got some useful hints to help you. Second – if after a great deal of soul-searching you really don't fancy learning the whole thing, you can still perform the vast majority of the pieces in this collection as dramatised readings. I've got some handy hints here, too!

To learn . . .

When you first look at a two- or three-page script, with the full knowledge that all the lines are yours, it can be rather a daunting prospect! At the end of the day, repetition and slog is what will finally make the script sink in, but there are some basic principles that can help in the process.

To begin, read the script over and over again. At this stage, don't even try to consciously learn it; just absorb it. The more you read it, the more you will start to automatically remember it and also sympathise with and gain an understanding of the character. It will also become more apparent how to phrase each line, pausing for effect, making the most of every nuance, and this will help develop how you play the character.

The temptation when reading through the script and rehearsing is to do it silently in your head – don't! As soon as you can, speak the words out loud; it's amazing how your brain becomes attuned to what you say. Of course at the outset you will make a hash of it, stumbling over the words and not making it sound remotely coherent, but this is what rehearsal is for. Please don't read it through a couple of times, get discouraged because it sounds less than perfect, then give up. A bit of old-fashioned patience will pay off. (This, I admit, sounds a bit rum coming from one who has regularly flung his script book across the room in an out-break of artistic temperament!)

By doing the above, rather than simply learning the words, you have acquired the thought process of the character by getting under their skin. In other words, you're trying not only to understand what they say, but what they're thinking too. This is the key to remembering the script.

To give an example, imagine telling a joke (if you don't tell jokes, bear with me for a minute). Telling a joke to a gathered crowd of listeners can often take a good few minutes. If you actually wrote the joke out as a script, word for word, in many cases it could cover a good page or so. (Not knock-knock jokes obviously, but you get the point!) Now, I guarantee when you tell a joke you pretty much tell it word for word, with minimal diversion from the 'script' – yet you've never actually learnt it! If you saw the joke as a page-long script, the thought of learning it would suddenly become a lot scarier! But the reason we don't have a problem is we're not remembering a bunch of words: we're remembering a story, a collection of images that is much harder to forget.

So, we need to apply this technique to learning a script. Yes, you're learning the words of course, but try also to learn the story in thoughts and images; this will help you naturally recall the words you have hammered into your brain.

The other advantage of learning the script rather than reading it is that it gives you freedom of movement. In this collection I decided to use very little in the way of stage direction in order to make the monologues as flexible as possible, but this doesn't mean you should stand stock still. At obvious breaks in the script, change position. Perhaps at one point you'll be standing centre stage enthusiastically building a narrative; at another time, the character may be better off sitting down, in a state of melancholic thought. By the way, line spaces in the text of the monologues indicate a brief pause for dramatic effect. You can also utilise a few basic props if you feel this helps, but this all becomes much more difficult if you haven't learnt the script.

I suppose the advantages and disadvantages of learning the script are pretty obvious! The advantage is it gives you greater flexibility, and it looks more impressive. The disadvantage is it calls for much more in the way of preparation and discipline. I prefer to learn monologues by heart, but the reality of life is that it's not always possible to do so. If you have to do a particular monologue at an event with so little time to spare that learning it is pretty much impossible, this does not mean you have to read it in a dull, lifeless way – on the contrary. Let's look at some ways you can perform monologues as dramatised readings and still make a strong impact.

. . . *Or not to learn*

One of my other books in the Great Ideas series is on dramatising Bible readings. This was in response to the times I've squirmed as people drone through the awesome power of the Scriptures, draining all life and verve from them. When we read a monologue from the page, we don't have to do so in a dull, lifeless way; we can still perform, giving the script real character and power.

Rule number one is this. If you decide not to learn the script, don't try to hide this from the audience. There is nothing so futile as having chunks of your script furtively hidden inside newspapers or stuck on tables (echoes of *The Generation Game*). Believe me, the audience will know! Why am I so sure? Because I've tried it and it's pretty pathetic! If you learn a piece, enjoy the freedom of having no script. If you use a script, be up front about it; the audience won't mind – if you perform the piece in a dramatic and engaging way.

Now we've got that basic pitfall out of the way, how do you begin to prepare a dramatised monologue reading? Well, to start with, begin exactly the same way as if you were learning it! Read the script over and over again (and a few more times, if at all possible!). Generally the aim is for you to pretty much know what's coming next without looking, even though you haven't strictly learnt it word for word. This gives you the freedom to look up with confidence, rather than reading with your head constantly down, looking at the script. Also, this familiarity with the script will obviously help with your general confidence and ability to make the character three-dimensional and believable. For many people, having the security of the script in front of them allows them to perform much better, as they have no niggling concerns that they will forget the next line.

If you decide to perform a monologue as a dramatised reading, still give yourself the discipline of some rehearsal, familiarising yourself with the script and character, and practising out loud. If you choose to perform a reading, but then don't bother to spend any time rehearsing it, the likelihood is that it won't be very impressive, or certainly not as impressive as it could have been.

Now of course, for one reason or another, we sometimes choose to do something at very short notice. In these cases, obviously, any kind of structured rehearsal is impossible, but these cases should be exceptional.

Once I was at a wedding, and at very short notice the person who was due to read the scripture pulled out with a terrible case of cold feet. I was asked to step in and read the passage, which I was happy to do. Fortunately enough, I was familiar with the scripture, which helped, but even so I was aware that reading it to the congregation after quickly whizzing through it a couple of times at the back of the church meant it could have been much better. People were very kind about my delivery of it, but in myself I knew that with a bit more time I could have done a better job.

So, with the exception of a last-minute change of plan, assuming we have some notice, let's be really diligent in our preparation. In the same way that I expect a preacher to have put time and thought into the sermon, the worship leader into the music, and the coffee maker into the creation of a perfect cup of coffee, I expect a reader or performer to have made some effort.

Where learning a piece gives you freedom of movement, reading a monologue doesn't have to mean you don't move. When I read a piece, I always ensure that the script is on a lectern of some sort, at the optimum height (for my fast-failing eyesight!), and that the sheets are all visible, to cut out any shuffling or turning over of pages. Although any major kind of movement is limited, you can still make basic movements where appropriate. Sometimes, though, movements can be distracting and the most powerful and effective thing to do is stand still. These things become apparent during your run-throughs, and it is also very helpful during a rehearsal to have a second person with you, acting as a 'director' to make constructive comments.

I hope some of these basic principles help you to get started. Nothing quite teaches you like putting it all into practice, and as you begin to perform, your appetite will be whetted to improve and learn as you go. I said earlier that I hoped the book contained something suitable for everyone, but it may be you need a piece for a very specific story or subject. This next section is just for you.

Writing your own

I would like to give any budding writers out there some brief encouragement to pick up their pens and have a go at scripting some monologues for themselves. Unfortunately, a talent for good writing is not possessed by all, but you won't know until you put pen to paper and try. I'm in no way at a place where I can offer a writing masterclass, but I can share with you some things that help me in putting a piece together.

For starters, be warned that it can be a very slow process. Sometimes the ideas flow freely and you can't write fast enough, but at other times it can be a real slog and you need to be very disciplined. If I only wrote when the muse descended I would rarely get anything done! Also, don't expect to get it right first time; my notebook is literally covered in huge crossings-out and scribbles.

Getting your inspiration needn't be an arduous task; in fact it can actually be great fun! Go and see as many plays as you can, read lots of good books and keep your eyes open for interesting current events in the newspapers. I'm not proposing that you plagiarise someone else's work, but taking in as many creative forms as possible will give you ideas for suitable content and styles that will work when employed on the stage.

Always think of your 'target audience' when writing. Are you aiming at 'clued-up' Christians, fringe people, seekers or the totally unchurched? Make sure you use language and situations that will be both familiar and accessible.

Choosing your character

As I said earlier, the joy of a biblical monologue is the incredible depth of choice the Scriptures offer. To start with, there are literally dozens of characters that are well known to everybody. You don't need to venture further than Genesis to discover Adam, Eve, Noah and Joseph . . . plus of course many other central characters who will be well known to Christians. Then, of course, you can have fun with Bible observers. Simply choose a story or event in the Bible, and imagine a fictional onlooker. These can make a great impact as you surmise what might go through the mind of a supposed observer at that time.

For a more contemporary piece, in the main I find that the topic I want to communicate comes first, then the character. Limitless ideas can be used, from moral belief to current issues facing society – take your pick! For the creation of your character, this is where 'people-watching' becomes a useful skill! An hour at a café, ambling round a local supermarket or walking down the high street should give you all the ammo you need for a new character. This, of course, is after you've exhausted all the odd foibles of your family, friends and folk from church! (Yes, dear friends, if you think you recognise someone in one of these monologues, you're probably right!)

Background study

In some cases this can take me as long as actually writing the piece. For contemporary pieces, it is of less importance, but some subjects may call for research. Either way, for monologues based on biblical characters or stories, in my opinion it is essential to do some background reading. A monologue isn't there simply to kill a bit of time in a service or raise a few chuckles: it can inform and challenge.

You can't possibly write a piece about a character without knowing about them. So, once you have made your choice, get a concordance or study aid, find all the passages where they make an appearance and get your facts straight. Note down any key events in their lives: where they are from, experiences they have had, their journey of faith, their strengths and weaknesses etc. As well as giving you stacks of ideas for what to put in the monologue, it makes for a really interesting study too. Many is the time that I have been researching for a monologue and learnt so much that I have used the information in the content of a sermon.

Once you have all the information, assemble what you decide to use into some kind of order. This then forms the framework for the monologue. With the confidence that you have some biblically based facts (some of which may not be very well known), you can fill in the gaps with a large dash of 'dramatic licence', making the piece relevant to your intended listeners.

It's hard to explain this further; best just to give it a go! As an example, read one of mine that is based on a real Bible character. Try to distinguish the fact from the fiction – it shouldn't be too difficult. The key thing is to try to make a point without drowning the true essence of the story.

In the beginning

With any piece of drama it is essential to have a strong start. This can be done in many ways; it doesn't necessarily have to be loud and in your face. Something that captures the audience's attention and makes them want to sit up and listen is the main aim.

This is the dual responsibility of the writer and performer. From a writing point of view, make sure the opening line is a good one. Don't make it really drab, but on the other hand you don't want to make a juicy point too early on, because you need the listeners to get warmed up and used to your character. As a very general rule, I tend to make the first few lines fun and engaging, then get on to the main substance of the story. For instance, Pilate's wife might spend a few lines complaining about husbands in general before letting on who her husband is, and at this point the main part of the monologue begins.

The end

If there's one thing more key than the opening, it's the close. What is it you want to say? What do you want to leave the audience thinking? That is what you need to answer when writing your close.

Sketches are traditionally difficult to finish. You get on a roll when writing the middle bit, then hit a brick wall. Where possible, it's good to decide in advance where you want to go with the piece. There is nothing more embarrassing for a performer than to do a piece with a painfully 'eggy' ending!

Again, as a general rule (which I often break!) the close is best as a more thought-provoking challenge. Even if the sketch has been quite light-hearted in its general content, to suddenly bring it round can be incredibly effective.

Brief as that is, I hope it gives you some encouragement to get stuck into the writing process. It is worthwhile to get someone whose opinion you trust to offer you thoughts and constructive criticism. I admit this can be tough when you've spent hours putting a piece together, but the fact is that there are times when something that seems incredibly funny as you write at your desk is a lame duck when you actually put it on the stage. (Believe me, I know!) Go forth and scribe, and I hope this collection gets you going.

EASTER

1. The Reliable Rock

'Then, in the distance – not nearby, but very
clearly – I heard the sound of the cock crow.'

PETER

Do you know what my name means?

And this is for real, not one of them made-up ones you get on a bookmark or on the side of a mug! No, this is straight from the original, ancient, foreign translation, right? It means 'rock'. Rock! Not bad, eh? Rock hard! Nails – that's what I am, mate – nails. Peter the rock – reliable, sturdy, fearless, unbreakable, un . . . shiftable. Basically, you'd be wise not to mess with me, right?

As far as the boss was concerned, I was his right-hand man, you know – not that he ever actually said that, not in so many words, like – but that was certainly how I saw it. And who could blame him if he did? I was always up for everything, me; first to volunteer every time. Bit impetuous, some might say, but there's far worse faults than that, in my book. Not like some of the others, with their lack of enthusiasm, moping and lollopping about. Not me – I was totally sold on him, prepared to go to the ends of the earth, to die if needs be.

Which is why on this particular day, it was such a shock when he said what he said.

* * *

He got us all together, we had supper, really nice time, and then he comes straight out with it: 'One of you will betray me.' Well, we all started looking at each other, furtively, thinking, 'Oh, please not me' . . . but of course it turns out that it's Judas!

Well, no surprise there, never trusted him much anyway, always a bit underhand for my liking – but that wasn't the end of it. We went out for a walk – well, the rest of us did – up the Mount of Olives, and that's when he said it: 'This very night you will all fall away on account of me.' This is getting ridiculous, I thought. All right, Judas maybe, but all of us? Me, the rock? I thought for a second maybe he was having a bit of a joke, 'cos Jesus has got a great sense of humour, you know. It's not often mentioned, but he can crack me up. But I could tell by his face this time he was being really serious.

I piped up first, as usual, and I was, like, no way! I said, 'The others might back down, Lord – the ditherers – but not me. I'll never fall away.' At this point the others kept quiet, wisely. Then Jesus looked at me and said, 'I tell you the truth. This very night, before the cock crows, you will disown me three times.' That took a moment to sink in. I'd never heard the like. Disown Jesus? Me, disown the Master? And three times! I mean, once is hard enough to believe, but three times! I was, like, 'No way! Even if I have to die with you, I will never disown you!' To give the other boys their credit, at this they all said the same, pledging their allegiance. But of course he knew . . . all along he knew.

Later that night, when he was arrested, I was still living up to my name. When Judas appeared, with a great crowd, all with their swords and clubs, he had the nerve to approach the Master, and as a final act of betrayal kiss him on the cheek. Seeing him standing there, holding his purse, jangling with his ill-gotten gains, I saw red, I did! One of the mob stepped forward to grab Jesus, and I got out my sword and took a swing. It wasn't my best effort, admittedly. I ended up taking off this bloke's ear, and there was absolute mayhem. But in the middle of it all, Jesus put us in our place. 'Put your swords away. All who draw the sword will die by the sword.' He looked over to me as if to say, 'If I want to get out of this, don't you think I can manage?' And I mean, of course he could. Then he let them take him away – no struggle, no clever argument, he just went. I looked back to take a last glance, and then I ran. I ran.

*　*　*

I don't know how far I ran, but it was a long way. I sat down on this low wall to take a breather, to try and work things out in my mind, and as I did, this servant girl came up to me – sweet little thing she was, can't have been more than 10 or 11 – and she says, 'You were with Jesus of Galilee.' 'I don't know what you're talking about,' I says, and shooed her away. But she comes back, this time with another girl, bit older, who looks at me like I'm a criminal or something, and says, 'Yeah, I saw you with that Jesus of Nazareth.' And again I said, ' I don't know the man, leave me alone!' I don't know why I said it. I was still trying to work things out in my mind, plan a course of action I suppose, but nobody would give me any peace and quiet.

And then a big group come towards me, all knowing and grinning, and the spokesman says, 'Surely you are one of them! Even your accent gives you away!' So I stood up and swore at them and yelled again and again, 'I don't know the man!'

* * *

Then, in the distance – not nearby, but very clearly – I heard the sound of the cock crow. And I wept.

The rock! Huh! Reliable, sturdy, fearless? What has become of me? What *will* become of me? What kind of a church is he going to build on a rock like me?

Bible reference: Matthew 26:69–75

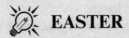 **EASTER**

2. The Greatest Mistake in History

'When man allows greed to take hold of him, he
is vulnerable to an act of bribery.'

JUDAS

Evil? Me? Well, maybe – I suppose it depends on your perspective. It's an understandable opinion, but are you sure you've been furnished with all the facts – the truth, the whole truth and nothing but the truth, as they say? Maybe. Maybe not – so you should listen.

For starters, think on this. I was, and I suppose to a certain extent I still am, one of the chosen twelve. The Master could have chosen anyone from literally thousands of possibles, but no, he chose me. Judas. Why? Hmm, why? If he knew what I was going to do, why did he choose me? For fun, for the challenge – or to fulfil his purpose? Or maybe he did not know that I would betray him. Maybe he made a mistake. Oh, but then there is a problem: the Master never makes mistakes. Faith in him is founded on his having no imperfections. So, there is our first dilemma. Why not choose someone like one of the other eleven saints? (Although they were far from perfect, let me tell you.) I admit I betrayed him, but all the others abandoned him in his hour of most need. Ah! But that is them; I must accept my position. I admit I did accept a bribe; I did betray my Master.

People curse me. They ask me, 'Judas, what reason did you have to betray him?' Reason? Well, that's easy. It wasn't personal: I loved him. He had always been so kind to me, shown me respect, given me responsibility, accepted me . . . No, the reason is a lot more basic – money. The root of all . . . ah, you know. The trouble with the Master is his perfection makes him so misunderstood. All of us have been guilty of misunderstanding him. I joined with him to lead a political rebellion, anarchy! Overturn our hopeless and corrupt government, create a new political order; net result – untold riches. Unfortunately the rebellion he spoke of was of a peaceful nature, the treasure of a heavenly kind. These things were not in my vocabulary. Not what I signed up for.

'Ah, but Judas,' the people say. 'You are a common thief; you had your hand in the purse of your friends for years.'

Yes, I took money. I accepted the bribery of my conscience, but was I not justified? How many of you would work for nothing? How many of you would go to your office or factory or field and at the end of the week expect to receive no money? (*JUDAS appears to see no hands raised among his listeners.*) Ah, none of you. Yes, I took money, but I worked my fingers to the bone for it. I took what I rightfully earned, and it was still a pittance.

When man allows greed to take hold of him, he is open; he is vulnerable to an act of bribery. How were the plans hatched? For me – one so close to the Master – it was simple, so simple. A dimly lit garden, an appointed hour, a Judas kiss . . . ah, it's history. Not only was I *being bribed*, I think I too was trying *to bribe*: trying to bribe the Master into using his power – force his hand, so to speak, into an act of rebellion. As the authorities came I thought maybe he would strike back – rebel against them, set into action the course of events I so longed for. Peter, impulsive as ever, struck first. Swish! He sliced an ear off one of the party; there was screaming, and blood everywhere. The Master, calmly as ever, reached over to touch the man. He was instantly healed. 'Put your sword away,' he said. 'All who draw the sword will die by the sword.' I knew then my dream was over. As he was led away we exchanged a glance – the final time he looked upon me – and I admit I felt a pang of guilt.

I should feel happy. Look what I'm left with: the bag of money – fully earned, untold riches. But now I have it, where do I go from here?

Bible reference: Matthew 26:14–16

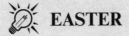 **EASTER**

3. Absolute Power

'Governor Pilate may *appear* to have the final say; *he* may even think he has the final say, if I do my job properly; but in reality he has no such thing.'

CAIAPHAS

A very common and, it has to be said, understandable misconception about power is that the top bod is in charge: the Prime Minister, el Presidente, the Governor – and of course it is the natural assumption. But no . . . invariably they are nothing more than a puppet, charged with the duty of safeguarding public perceptions. They're often put in place thanks merely to a winning smile, a pretty wife or a mane of trustworthy silver hair. But if you want to pinpoint where the real power is, where the decisions are made, you need to look down a rung: to who briefs the top bod, who puts the words in their mouths – the advisors, the press secretaries, the spin doctors and, of course, the High Priests.

And it's no different here in Judea from anywhere else. Governor Pilate may *appear* to have the final say; *he* may even think he has the final say, if I do my job properly; but in reality he has no such thing! Of course we indulge various of his inconsequential whims and fancies. That adds nicely to the illusion that he's in charge. But when it comes to things that are really important – well, then he's left in no doubt on which side his bread is buttered. On these points of fact I will have my way.

Take this Jesus character. To be honest I took an instant dislike to him, right from day one. No, more than a dislike; an intense hatred. I mean – how dare he cross me? High Priest Caiaphas, educated and wealthy! Leader of the élite Saducees, charged with upholding the religiosity of the region. And him, a useless carpenter from goodness only knows where, wandering around with his rag tag mob of oddballs and misfits. Really, the competition was always woefully unfair!

But give him some credit, I suppose. With his popularist message of the poor being rich and the low being high, he did manage to attract quite some following. Well, the idea of a kingdom in which the leaders served the masses – he couldn't lose, could he? Though personally I couldn't imagine a manifesto with less appeal. And don't think this was the first time this sort of thing had happened. No – it was a pretty regular occurrence. But in the past I'd always managed to nip it in the bud, chop down the said party before they hit their prime. But this one slipped through my fingers somehow. Maybe I underestimated him.

Sad, really – it was never a question of *whether* this Jesus should die or not, just a matter of *how* and *when*! And with all the red tape nowadays, that's when things get really tricky. How do you get your man and cover your own back at the same time? It's not easy.

Then we met Judas – a snivelling mess of a man, but we needed someone on the inside. So we told him how important he was, and what a key role he could play, as well as offering financial compensation, of course. And he took it, sold his lofty principles for a paltry bag of silver and a few choice compliments – pathetic! And so it was that I met this Jesus, face to face in my courtroom.

Now, in a situation like this, evidence is what you need – hard evidence. You can't just go around killing people for no apparent reason. There needs to be order, or at least the perception of order. We had nothing, or very little. Yes, there were a few false witnesses, some of whom we'd paid, regaling the court with far from solid testimony, contradicting each other half the time, but there was nothing that would hold up, allowing us to keep face while sticking in the knife. And then two people came forward, and looking right at Jesus they said, 'This fellow, he said he was able to destroy the temple of God and rebuild it in three days.' There was a collective sharp intake of breath, followed by low murmuring. Jesus remained absolutely silent. I said to him, 'Well, what about it? Did you say that or didn't you?' Still silence. So I said, 'I charge you, under oath by the Living God, tell us if you are the Christ, the Son of God.' And then out of the very mouth of the soon-to-be-slaughtered lamb came all the evidence I could need. 'Yes, it is as you say. And in the future you will see me, the Messiah, sitting at the right hand of God and returning on the clouds of heaven.'

Bingo! I could hardly contain my joy. But I put on my stoniest expression, tore at my robe and shouted, 'Blasphemy! He has spoken blasphemy! What need have we of any other witnesses? You have all heard him say it! What is your verdict?' And they were unanimous in their declaration of 'Death! He is worthy of death.'

Of course, my council has no official power in this regard: a death sentence needs to be approved by Rome. No, I am a High Priest, a man of God – I have no part in such sordid matters, officially. Which brings me back to where I began, to dear Pilate, our esteemed Governor. He must finally approve our verdict, sign on the dotted line. And I fear he won't be too happy. He has a rather soft centre when it comes to such things. But I will explain to him that there is no other way; no other way to appease the people, to avoid upheaval and bloodshed. Allow one man to die, I'll say, or the whole nation will perish. Yes, he will see the logic – reluctantly, maybe. But on this point of fact I will have my way.

* * *

It's very nice, isn't it, to have high moral principles? Most laudable. But they can be costly – perhaps too costly. And in all events order must be maintained. We simply cannot accommodate would-be messiahs challenging our authority.

But what if he really was the Messiah? Well then, he'll be back, won't he? Returning on the clouds of heaven. But things like that just don't happen – do they, now?

Bible reference: John 11:45–57

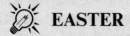 **EASTER**

4. The Unfair Reprieve

'I consider myself a man of morals. It's a weird
kind of morality, I know, but there you go.'

BARABBAS

Trouble's always been my middle name – ever since I was a kid. I've always been the rebellious type. Can't help it. Must be part of my genetic pool or something. If someone bosses me around, tells me I've got to do such-and-such or be in a certain place, I'm overcome with this unquenchable desire to do the exact opposite, you know? And it's got me in trouble, ooh, on numerous occasions. I've been had up for sedition, conspiracy to overthrow, GBH and even murder. Now, don't get me wrong – that's not my first choice, murder, no. Only for consideration in extreme circumstances. But believe me, sometimes it's the only way to get a message through to these blockheaded Romans. I mean, I consider myself a man of morals. It's a weird kind of morality, I know, but there you go.

Anyway, this particular time I was seriously up to my neck in it. They'd banged me up with a list of charges as long as my arm. Enemy number one I was, and there was only going to be one possible outcome. My number was up, if you catch my drift. But then I was thrown a lifeline – not much of one, I grant you, but at least something, I thought. I was told that Governor Pilate's custom during the Passover celebrations was to release one Jewish prisoner to the people – anyone they wanted. And this year, apparently, it was between me and Jesus, the so-called King of the Jews.

Well, that's that, I thought. I've got no chance against him – Mr Popular, with his healings and his miracles and his message of love and forgiveness. I'll be like a lamb to the slaughter. But maybe it's justice, I thought. In his own way maybe he's having more effect than I am. I knew all about him. I'd been following his progress, at a distance – I didn't want to get too involved. I had my own political agenda to follow, and it was more 'overthrow and rule' than 'love and serve'. Still, I thought, if I can just get to speak at least a few words to him before they set him free – tell him to make the most of it, his freedom, make them pay – then I could still serve one final purpose. Of course I never got the chance.

So the time comes for the people to choose one of us to get the chop. From my cell I could hear the crowd gather. I couldn't see anything, but it sounded pretty sizeable. Then followed the muffled sound of Governor Pilate's voice, droning on as usual, using twenty words where one would do. But then the clear sound of the crowd, one voice in perfect unison, screaming 'Barabbas, Barabbas, BARAAABBAS!' That'll be me then, I thought. After the screams died down, Pilate spoke again. Still couldn't hear what he was saying – too far away – but once more the crowd were unified and delivered their verdict with cruel conviction – 'Crucify him . . . Crucify him . . . Crucify him!'

Pandemonium broke out. The crowd were uncontrollable, probably drunk, but I was alone with my thoughts. I knew one day it would end for me, probably messily, maybe heroically even, but not like this. Not like this.

Time passed – not long, just a few short minutes, I think – and then one of the guards appeared. He was looking at me, smiling sarcastically, swinging his chain of keys around – I'd have liked to wrap them round his neck. He came into the cell, bent over and unlocked the shackles from my feet and hands. I froze. Thoughts rushed through my head, thoughts of striking out, taking down the aggressor and making my escape – but in that split second the guard said to me, 'You are free to go.' There must be a catch, I thought, some sick game maybe. But no. Again he said it, 'You are free to go.'

I turned to him. 'But I heard my name,' I said. 'The crowd, they called my name.' 'They were calling for your release.' The explanation registered slowly, and then again I protested: 'But they cried "Crucify him!" I heard it – "Crucify him!"' 'That was for the other one: Jesus, the King of the Jews.' 'Why? What did he do to them that was so terrible?' The guard shrugged, uninterested. 'I don't know, do I? And if I were you, I wouldn't ask too many questions.'

To this there was nothing more to say. So I left, a free man.

* * *

A reprieve is a strange thing, don't you think? Imagine going to the doctor for some tests or whatever, and he writes to you with the results. Terrible news: it's incurable. You have a matter of weeks to live, to sort out your affairs. Then the next day he contacts you: there's been the most terrible mix-up. It was all a mistake. You're perfectly healthy; you'll live a normal life. What a sense of relief!

Do you think about the other person? The one who was told that their tests were clear. The one who had a wild party with their family and friends to celebrate. Then the next day, it's the doctor again: there's been the most terrible mix-up and things aren't so rosy in the garden.

These are the confusing thoughts that keep me awake every night.

* * *

After I was released, I stayed around, disguising myself as best I could. I watched them drag him into the courtyard and flog him, countless times. And I thought it should have been me.

I saw them spitting and jeering at him, placing a crown of thorns on his head. And I thought it should have been me.

Then I saw them bang in the nails, lift him up on the tree for all to see. And I thought it should have been me.

And even now, all this time later, when I consider all the events of that day, I still can't help thinking it should have been me. It should have been me.

Bible reference: Matthew 27:15–26

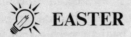 **EASTER**

5. A Dirty Job

'When they're handed over to me, the deal is done
– they are criminals, murderers, terrorists. Don't
blame me. I'm not the judge and jury.'

CENTURION

People often say to me, 'How do you do what you do? Ooh, *I* couldn't – it would make my stomach turn!' And I say to them, 'Listen, it's a dirty job but someone's got to do it.' I mean, they make their sly little comments, but it's 'cos of the likes of me that they can sleep a bit easier at night. And to be honest, the money's not bad either, but that's only a secondary concern. I heard recently that some old historian fella described it as '*Mors turpissima crucis*' or something like that . . . which means 'the most terrible way to die'. And it is. Crucifixion is the most terrible way to die.

More than that, it's barbaric. It's not just a case of hanging on a tree for a bit. No, it's the whole package. It starts with total humiliation. The victims are stripped and paraded. Then the soldiers whip them with leather straps studded with thorns or sharp bits of bone. Some of the soldiers even have lumps of lead specially embedded into their whips – the really sick ones, like. Oh, and they're given every opportunity to indulge in acts of sadism and gratuitous vulgarity. Every latent, inhuman desire is given free rein during the flogging. Makes you shudder.

Next, the newly scourged victim has to cart his cross to the place of his own execution; there's some sort of ironic poetry in that, I suppose. And then it's actually attaching them to the cross, which is where I come in.

You can go one of two ways. The first is to just bind them tightly to the horizontal beam of the cross; it's the less painful of the two options, but more time-consuming, death normally taking a good few days. Alternatively we can use nails.

Now, if any of you are squeamish, block your ears at this point, right! We put one nail in here, just below the wrist, and a second at the same point on the other arm. We then attach the horizontal beam to the vertical one, which is already in place. Then for the killer blow: to stop the legs kicking around, we hold both feet together and secure them in place with one final nail. In these instances death is normally a matter of hours rather than days, what with all the pain and the loss of blood and difficulty in breathing.

Yeah, crucifixion is, without a doubt, barbaric.

But who am I to comment? It's the Roman way to deal with a problem. As far as I'm concerned, when they're handed over to me, the deal is done – they are criminals, murderers, terrorists. Don't blame me. I'm not the judge and jury, I make no moral judgements. Can't afford to. A centurion with a conscience! That makes for a very deadly cocktail. My predecessor always taught me, 'Never get involved emotionally! Keep your head down and do your job. Never listen to the claims of a condemned man – they'll mess with your brain.' And it's never been a problem; I'm known for my dogged professionalism. And then came last Friday . . .

The paperwork came through for this guy – a carpenter by trade, but apparently some kind of enemy of the state. I'd heard some stuff about him, mixed reports – sounded like he'd fallen foul of the powers that be. The talk was his trial had been farcical. Now, I'm a man of justice so I wasn't happy about that, but I still had a job to do. So, we laid him out, arms outstretched, as is the norm, and I banged in the nails.

Now, I've trained myself over many years not to listen to a word they say. They can scream, they can plead innocence, they can curse, and I will literally not hear a thing. But this carpenter, he really didn't say a thing, not a whimper; didn't even make a movement as I drove in the nails. And as a victim's cries usually fall on my deaf ears, so his silence screamed at me with a deafening force. I never make eye contact with the victims – another thing they teach you – but with this carpenter I couldn't help myself. And as I looked in his eyes I saw no animosity, no hatred – just understanding, compassion. I ordered the bar to be put in place and, as quickly as I could, head down, I held his feet in place and banged in the final nail.

And then I heard him say, 'Father, forgive them, for they don't know what they are doing.'

I can cope with the curses, the verbal and physical abuse, the hatred – but what I cannot cope with is forgiveness. Undeserved forgiveness.

* * *

I stood at the foot of the cross, frozen in my position, even after my shift was finished.

I stood at the foot of the cross as the sky turned dark as deepest night, in the middle of the day.

I stood at the foot of the cross as the carpenter cried, '*Eloi, Eloi, lama sabachthani*?' My God, my God, why have you forsaken me? And as he sighed his last he cried out, 'It is finished.'

I stood at the foot of the cross while some of the soldiers checked for any slight reaction from his lifeless body. There was none.

I stood at the foot of the cross and said, just to myself, 'Truly he was the Son of God.'

* * *

And his followers, they now claim he is risen. His enemies are desperately trying to explain away an empty tomb. And me? Well, what future is there for me, the man who killed the Son of God? I wonder just how far his forgiveness will stretch.

Bible reference: Matthew 27:45–54

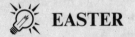 **EASTER**

6. Honestly Doubtful

'"When I place my hands into his side, then I'll believe." That shut them all up! Yeah, I admit I doubted, but I wanted to believe.'

THOMAS

I'll let you all into a little secret. After much mind-bending cogitation I've worked out what the single most annoying phrase in the English language is. Are you ready? – 'Ooh, you had to be there!' 'Ooh, you had to be there!' Any time anybody says it to me I have this sudden urge to whack them over the head with a blunt instrument! Well, it's so mind-numbingly infantile. And it's always preceded by some witless individual recounting a fantastical tale of such hilarity or such awesome nature that all those who were present at the event are worked up into a dizzied frenzy!

And then there's you: the odd one out. Intently listening with a totally bored and blank expression on your face, wondering if you were even born on the same planet as this inane bunch of muppets! Then it comes, that phrase of such annoyingly patronising qualities: 'Ooh, you had to be there!' 'Ooh, Thomas, you had to be there!'

And of course, as you can imagine, it happened to me, just the other week. And you know, it's so infuriating, 'cos usually I'm always around – Mr Reliable, me. But just this once, *just this once*, I'd popped out. What with all the upset of our leader's death, morale in the camp was a bit low. So I took it upon myself to go into town and buy a ticket for the Jerusalem lotto. Sad, I know. I never usually bother: the whole thing's rigged by Caiaphas and his cronies anyway, but it was a double rollover week, so I thought to myself, 'Why not – why not!' A bit of hope amidst all the hopelessness! Anyway, when I got back the place was in uproar; people crawling on the ceiling.

'What's going on?' I asked. 'He came back.' 'What?' 'He came back!' 'Who are you talking about?' I asked. 'The Lord. We have seen the Lord!' I waited for the punchline but it wasn't forthcoming. 'Where?' I says. 'Here.' 'Here?! When?' 'Just now.'

I mean, isn't it just typical? I admit I was doubtful, extremely doubtful. Well, it's hardly surprising, when you

46

consider the events of the last few days. It was a highly dubious tale. I was expecting Peter or James to suddenly jump up and say, 'Ah ha, not really – only kidding!' And I didn't want to look too gullible. I do have some pride, you know. But they didn't. They were all too busy maniacally jumping around. This previously fearful pack of scared little rabbits was totally transformed. I mean, you had to see them yourself to believe it. 'Ooh, Thomas,' they said, 'you had to be there!'

And of course that just about did it for me. That pushed me over the precipice: 'Oh, I'll believe,' I told them. 'I'll believe when I see the nail wounds in his hands and put my fingers into them. When I place my hand into his side, then I'll believe.' That shut them all up! Yeah, I admit I doubted, but I wanted to believe. I truly wanted to believe.

The next week or so was tough, really tough. I wanted what all the others had but I couldn't quite grasp hold of it. And I'd loved the Lord, oh yeah. Just a while before, I'd been willing to walk into the jaws of death with him, but this – I just couldn't get my head round it.

And then he appeared. In that same room. Don't know how – the doors were all locked – but there he was standing there. He looked right at me. He knew. He knew what I'd said about wanting to put my hands into his wounds. And he offered. 'Put your fingers into my hands. Put your hand into my side. Don't be faithless any longer. Believe.'

And I could have touched those wounds, but I didn't. Didn't need to. I just said, 'My Lord and my God.' Not particularly original, maybe, but succinct and to the point. The others looked on smiling. I thought, 'If any of them dare says "I told you so", I'll swing for them' . . . but they didn't.

* * *

So am I ashamed of my doubts? Not really – they served a purpose, caused me to question. Much better to have honest

47

doubts than feign certainty just to go along with the crowd, I reckon. And he understood that; I believe he understood.

Oh, and I nearly forgot to say: after all that, I lost – the lottery, I mean. No numbers at all, not one. I'm telling you – don't trust it. The whole thing's one big fix.

Bible reference: John 20:24–31

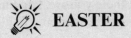 **EASTER**

7. The First Evangelist

'I know what you're thinking – "Crazy woman!
She's totally lost her marbles."'

MARY

I'm not a complicated person, me. No – in fact, some might say I'm a bit simple, childlike. Maybe it's true to a degree. I try to be as genuine as I can; and when it comes to the Master I'm eager to believe, obey, understand. Not sure quite how successful I am, but there you are. I do know that he changed my life, totally. Gave me a freedom I could never have hoped for.

I know what folk say about me: 'Oh, that Mary of Magdala was this, and Mary of Magdala does that!' But you shouldn't believe everything you read in the papers or hear in the market place – believe me, I should know!

Yes, he gave me everything, and in return my desire was to give him everything I could – everything.

And that's why I was there, with my friend Mary – another Mary. There at the place called Calvary; there at a distance when they cruelly lifted him onto that cross, the man I so innocently loved. I was there as always, prepared to tend to his every need, but of course there was nothing I could do, nothing anyone could do.

And later we were at the tomb, where a rich man (from Arimathea, I believe) took Jesus's body, wrapped it in a clean linen cloth and placed it in his own tomb, prepared for his own personal use and newly cut from the rock. And as the huge stone was rolled in front of the tomb's entrance, we sat opposite watching, waiting for . . . I don't know what.

As I returned home later that day, I can't explain the emotion I was feeling. I was numb, totally numb. I've suffered many things in my life, but nothing has come even close in comparison to this. At home I didn't know what to do with myself. I couldn't eat. I barely slept a wink. But I think I can recall a certain peace, some feeling of comfort. Of course this could be with the benefit of hindsight, with the knowledge I now have of the next chapter, so to speak.

On the Sunday morning, Mary and I decided to return to the tomb, just to take a look, really. We carried some spices in case there was an opportunity to embalm the body. What happened, though, was beyond belief. Suddenly the earth shook and the stone covering the tomb rolled back, apparently on its own. Then, bathed in a blinding light, an angelic being appeared, sitting on the stone, smiling down at us without a care in the world.

And I know what you're thinking – 'Crazy woman! She's totally lost her marbles!' And the thought probably would have occurred to me too, but for the fact I was so petrified. Even worse than Mary and I were these two brave and burly guards! Shaking like leaves, the pair of them were, scared to death, wearing the grey pallor of corpses!

Then, in all the excitement, the angel spoke: 'Do not be afraid, for I know you are looking for Jesus, who was crucified. He is not here; he has risen, just as he said.'

And he had said that he would rise – on numerous occasions, if memory serves. But I didn't think he meant it, not literally – none of us did. I just assumed it was a picture, an allegory. He was always telling us these cryptic stories with heavenly meanings. To be honest, a lot of them went over my head. And as these thoughts rushed through my mind, I looked into the tomb, and I could see the body was gone. The angel continued, 'See the place where he lay. Go and tell the disciples he has risen from the dead; he will go ahead of you into Galilee. There he will see you.'

So off we hurried, Mary and I – not the guards, they were still frozen with fear. And we were afraid, yet excited. And as I rushed off through the area where the tomb was, I bumped into this guy, a gardener, and I said something to him – can't remember what, and in the state I was in it probably made little or no sense. And this gardener just looked at me and simply said, 'Mary.'

And I knew then; in an instant I knew. So I replied, 'Master.'

'Do not be afraid,' he said. 'Go and tell my brothers to go to Galilee; there they will see me.'

So I did. I ran as fast as my legs could carry me. And I told them. I told them, 'I have seen the Lord.' And their response was – well, their response is another story for another time. But they did see him again, all of them.

And I stand amazed at my part in this tale. Me, Mary of Magdala, the first to see the resurrected Christ; the first to pass on the message of the resurrected Christ. Me! It always has been, and always will remain, totally beyond belief.

Bible reference: John 20:10–18

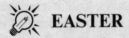 **EASTER**

8. Twenty-Four-Hour Guard

'Exactly what happened I can't explain. I'm a bit
woolly on the details, having fainted out of
sheer terror!'

GUARD

I've been given some right weird jobs in my time. As a temple guard it's par for the course, I suppose. But this one! Well, this job just about took the biscuit! I mean, I'm used to guarding just about everything, me: prisoners, of course – your murderers, thieves, fraudsters; the governor himself; the governor's wife; even the governor's wife's prize-winning poodle, Smudge! All of them at one time or another have come under my protection or guard, and understandably so. But a dead body – no joke, a dead body! Now that was a first.

The boss calls me up: 'Got a little job for you and another one of the boys, guarding a tomb. Likely to be about a three-day job.' So I asks, 'Ooh, what's in the tomb then, eh? Some long-lost treasure worth millions of shekels?' 'No,' he says. 'It's a dead body. We want to make sure it doesn't escape!'

Well, of course, it's understandable, isn't it? I mean, dead bodies are for ever doing a runner, aren't they? You've got to keep them in check or before you know it you'll have zombies wandering around all over the shop!

Anyway, he goes on to say that this dead guy, Jesus, had spouted off some old flannel about rising from the dead after three days, so it was just a precautionary measure. Well, I thought, mine is not to reason why, mine is just to do – so I called up my partner, Jimmy, and we hotfooted it down to this tomb. At least, we thought, it would be a nice, easy three days' work. Well, that's what we thought.

And it did start off very calmly. We got down there and not only did they have us on 24-hour guard, just to be really sure they'd rolled this huge stone in front of the entrance and sealed the tomb. No cracks or crevices visible, completely airtight. Neither were there any crowds to control, no religious fanatics, no paparazzi, no one. Well, except these two women who would occasionally come down and sit opposite the tomb, just staring and snivelling into their Kleenex. And that was it. Night and day, that was it – boredom personified.

But then it happened. Exactly what happened I can't

explain. I'm a bit woolly on the details, having fainted out of sheer terror! Both of us did – poor old Jimmy was catatonic! What I do remember, though, is the earth shaking, and a light, a really bright light. Then the stone slowly rolling back, like a giant wheel, and seated on top of it a celestial being! The two women were there as well, the snivellers. It looked like they were speaking to this creature – no idea what they was saying – and shortly after they ran off. Not a word to us, I hasten to add. They just ran off and left us.

But the most important thing I remember is the tomb; inside the tomb – it was empty. This Jesus we was supposed to be guarding was gone. Either they'd sealed up a totally empty tomb or . . . well, you tell me.

As soon as Jimmy and I got over our dazed and confused state, we went straight to the city to report what we'd witnessed to the chief priests. We told them everything: the earthquake, the light, the stone, the angel, the empty tomb – everything except the fainting in terror, of course. Well, I've got a reputation to keep. Anyway, they shoved us into this poky little room while they mulled over their options; hours they kept us waiting, devising a cunning plan. And after all that, you'll never guess what they came up with: the best they could manage with all their combined brainpower was that the disciples stole away Jesus's body in the dead of night and – wait for it – while we were asleep! Can you believe the cheek of it?

'No, no, no,' I says. 'I'm not having that put down on my CV. I've got a wife and four kids to support. I can't afford to be nicknamed the sleeping policeman. No, I'm sorry, you'll have to come up with something much better than that.'

So eventually they agreed to make it worth our while. They crossed our palm with a very generous amount of silver, and promised to intercede for us if the report of our 'slumber' came to the attention of the governor. When the story came out, I even got in the newspaper, picture and all, right-hand profile. My mum was very proud. And the cover-up worked!

The story stuck. It was circulated, and will continue to be for a very long time, I've no doubt.

* * *

The only problem is, I know it's not true. There were no disciples there, no bodysnatching – I know what I saw. And what I saw was nothing, emptiness . . . an empty tomb. And it makes me wonder. It just makes me wonder.

Bible reference: Matthew 27:62–28:15

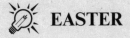 **EASTER**

9. The Interrogation

'I suppose you find me rather intimidating. Don't
worry – it's common. People always find me
intimidating. It comes with the job.'

Props

Desk and two chairs
Pen and paper
Bottle and glass
Bowl and water

Sound
Slow-tempo music

Introduction

This piece is essentially a monologue, although you will need a second person to play the role that is later revealed to be Jesus. The person playing this part has only one short line to say.

The piece is set in Pilate's office as he interrogates Jesus before making his judgement. It is important to communicate in the performance that, although it looks like the prisoner should be intimidated, it is in fact the other way round. Pilate is desperately trying to play the aggressor, but his attempts are failing.

This piece should be well rehearsed and needs to maintain a real, intense mood, even though it is fairly slow-moving.

(*PILATE sits at a desk writing, music is playing, and he is in deep thought.*)

PILATE: Send him in.

(*JESUS enters, head low, arms chained. He stays standing.*)

PILATE: Well . . .Well, well, well. So here you are. In the flesh, so to speak. (*PILATE goes to JESUS and lays his hands on his shoulders.*) Made of flesh. Born of flesh?

I've been looking forward to meeting you. Well, that's not entirely true, I suppose. Not looking forward to. You've become a bit of a pain in the

58

backside, to be totally honest. No, it's more that you've engaged my interest. My curiosity. I'm an incredibly curious person.

Do take a seat. (*PILATE pours himself a drink; JESUS remains standing.*) Sit. (*JESUS still stands.*) Please . . . (*JESUS sits.*) Thank you. That's better, isn't it? Much more comfortable to be sitting. Adopting a more relaxed tone. Less of that fidgeting and nervousness . . . Good. (*PILATE sits.*)

I suppose you find me rather intimidating. Don't worry – it's common. People always find me intimidating. All people find me intimidating. It comes with the job, I'm afraid; the position, you understand. I try to put people at their ease, offer them a seat, a drink maybe . . . (*Pours another drink*) Always helps to calm the nerves, wouldn't you say, a spot of the old Dutch courage? (*PILATE sits and drinks, wandering off into his own thoughts.*)

What was that? I'm sorry, did you say something? No?

Listen to me going on! I have a habit of doing that, I'm afraid. I'm sure people would stop me, but they're too scared of what I might do if they did – stop me, I mean, interrupt me. Oh, you know what I mean! Yes, my powers are far-reaching, very far-reaching, incredibly far-reaching.

By the way, I meant to ask: are you hurt? Were you injured in any way during transit? The guards can be rather overzealous at times in the pursuit of their tasks. Totally illegally, I hasten to add, but what can you do? (*JESUS rolls up sleeves. PILATE examines JESUS's arms.*) Ah, from the shackles. Ooh, it's cut through the skin! We should have it seen to, strictly speaking, if we were going by the book. But is there really any point?

Funny, really: however often I see injuries,

however insignificant they may be, I recoil. That may seem like a strong word, but I do, I recoil. Imagine, one such as I, squeamish – hard to believe, isn't it? Hard to believe when you consider my duty in this regard – the full-ranging implications of my jurisdiction. Of course it appals me, what I'm asked to do, but there you have it. One can't shirk one's role. One's role as God. My role as God. The power over life and death.

(*Pause.* PILATE *pours another drink.*)

Do you mind if I have another drink? Thank you. What was I saying? Oh yes. My role as God, life and death. Of course, death is never my first consideration. The last resort, in actual fact. I'd hate you to think I casually order my animals to kill people at the mere drop of a hat! No! But sometimes, and it pains me to say it, it is unavoidable. The only possible way to achieve . . . equilibrium. But believe me, it's the last resort . . . You do believe me? (*JESUS stares at* PILATE.)

There are many possible rungs on the ladder. A flogging, maybe. Bone-encrusted whips tearing huge chunks of flesh from the back, ribcage visible – that can sometimes appease. How does that sound? Better than it looks, I assure you. A lot better than it feels, I presume, from the screams. I've ordered mutilations, when people have forced me to. Oh, the stories I could tell you! You can see some of them for yourself, in the streets, reduced to begging for alms. But at least they have life. This I spared them . . . This I can spare *you*, if only you will allow me. Not only have you provoked my curiosity, but also my sympathy.

Understand, we live in political times. The

nation's gone crazy for political correctness. It's just not the done thing to claim you're the Son of God, even if it's true. Particularly if it's true, maybe. Can you see my predicament? I can play God; you cannot. That's politics. It's my job, not yours. I don't have to be your tormentor. I can be your . . . Saviour. If you'll allow me.

Look at me . . . Please, look at me. (*JESUS looks at PILATE.*)

Are you really the Son of God, the King of the Jews?

JESUS: (*Pause*) Yes, it is as you say.

PILATE: Then God help you. I cannot defend a man who will not hold up a defence for himself.
How will you answer all their accusations?
Will you not speak?
Do you understand what you will force me to do – hand you over to them? *To them!*

*   *   *

Don't make me wash my hands of you. Don't make me wash my hands of this whole situation. If you do, I promise it will be bad for you. It will be very bad. . .

(*PILATE and JESUS stare at each other. Music plays as lights fade to blackout. After a brief pause, lights come up. JESUS has exited and PILATE is seen crying as he washes his hands in a bowl. Lights fade to blackout.*)

Bible reference: Luke 23:1–25

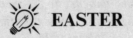 **EASTER**

10. The Last Temptation

'Here I am. Come and stand alongside me.
Come down!'

Introduction

I originally wrote this piece for two performers, but fairly quickly it became apparent it worked better as a monologue with the performer playing Satan actually speaking the words of Jesus, allowing the audience to create an image of the crucified Christ in their minds. Sounds confusing? It isn't!

The setting is Satan desperately trying to persuade Christ to come down from the cross, tempting him with all the kinds of things we would be susceptible to. To help the audience understand the different characters, you simply need to slightly alter your voice, manner or position. With some practice, this piece will prove highly effective.

(*As JESUS*) My Father, if it is possible, let this cup be taken away from me! But I want your will to be done, not mine.

* * *

(*Becomes mocking crowd*) Here, look at the sign: 'This is the king of the Jews'!

Ooh yes, we salute you, your Majesty!

He said he could destroy the temple and build it again in three days!

Well then, he'd better come down off the cross – if he's the Son of God, that is!

Yeah, he's the big cheese at saving others, but he can't save himself, can he?

All talk and no action – look at him! It's pathetic, totally pathetic!

* * *

(*Becomes SATAN. Claps hands slowly*) Ignorant fools! They have no idea what or whom they are dealing with . . . Do they? . . . Do they, Jesus? Jesus? Ah, there you are! Hello – I think you know who I am. In your time of deepest pain and loneliness, I thought I'd come to you, in true friendship, you understand. I sincerely mean that. I have the greatest respect for you. For your power.

The power to click your fingers and have legions of angels come down and rescue you. Believe me, you can finish this thing, this pain . . . and I know it hurts, really bad.

These ignorant fools – they don't deserve you. They reject you, they curse you. Come down! Come down and stand alongside me – the only one that's here in your hour of need. Everyone else, well, they've all disappeared, scarpered! Come on!

No? Stubborn as ever.

(*SATAN sits down in a storytelling mode.*)

Let me tell you a little story. There was a man, a great man. He was well respected and loved, but his obsession with his spiritual deity spoiled the wonderful human being he undoubtedly was. The obsession nearly drove him to the most cruel death imaginable, but at the last moment, as if by a spark of true inspiration, he saw sense, saw what he was doing to those people around him who loved him, and so he saved his life and put an end to his childish obsession.

Well, the people's love and respect for him grew. He fell in love with a beautiful woman, they had children, and those children grew up to love him and be like him. His life was inspirational; people were inexplicably drawn to him and his wonderful, humane qualities. You could even say he changed people's lives.

He lived to be a ripe old age and he died peacefully, in his own bed, surrounded by those who loved him most. What more could any man want? (*Stands again*) This could be your destiny – perfection.

(*As JESUS*) *Eloi, Eloi, lama sabachthani?* My God, my God, why have you forsaken me?

(*As SATAN, urgently*) He has! He has forsaken you! But I have not – here I am. Come, stand alongside me, come down! Come down!

(*As JESUS*) It is finished.

(*SATAN walks out in despair.*)

Bible references: Matthew 4:1–11; 26:39; 27:35–53

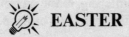 **EASTER**

11. The Note

'My days are busy enough as it is, with
manicures, pedicures and follicle treatments,
without having to concern myself
with matters of state!'

MRS PILATE

I'm sure you've all heard of that expression, 'the long-suffering wife'. Some of you may even think that description fits you to a T, and by the looks of it you could be right! But it can describe no one any better than it describes me. Look up the word 'long-suffering' in the dictionary and you'll find a picture of me, with furrowed brow, peering up from the page!

Of course, if you ask my husband about this, he'll paint you a very different picture. Behind my back I know he calls me everything under the sun – the old trouble and strife, the ball and chain, the fire-breathing dragon or just plain old battleaxe! And it's all so unfair, and highly inaccurate.

I admit we argue. All the time we argue, and over the most petty things – toilet seats, toothpaste tubes, the TV remote, you name it. And the annoying thing is – typical man – he always thinks he's right. Of course he very rarely is, because I normally am!

Stubborn! That's the best way to describe him. Stubborn as a mule. I suppose it's a natural by-product of having so much power. And power is a commodity he has in spades. Probably one of the reasons I love him.

* * *

The great Governor Pilate, my husband. Roman governor of an occupied and very reluctant Judea. But he's tough. He takes no prisoners, always speaks his mind, whoever you are. He's always had this habit of knocking people's noses out of joint.

The Jewish people here don't like him at all. He's managed to deeply offend all their religious leaders one way or the other. What they don't realise is, with him it's nothing personal; he's horrible to everybody. He believes a Roman conqueror should be treated with respect, and it's sparked off a fair few riots.

What he does struggle with is all the politics. The political wranglings. Whatever way you turn, there's a deal to be struck, an angle to be sussed, a situation to be manipulated or wangled. And it gets him down. He likes things to be upfront and in your face, none of this hush-hush stuff where you don't know if you're coming or going. But it's just not the way they play the game here.

* * *

Anyway, the whole thing has just come to a head. All over a seemingly inconsequential prisoner, a carpenter by the name of Jesus. Some bods from one of the religious councils wanted him to be sentenced to death, but they needed the governor's signature before it was a done deal. Well, for whatever reason, Pilate got the bit between his teeth and decided this Jesus was innocent of all charges, so he refused to sign the warrant. Why he made such a stand I'll never know. The easiest thing would have been to sign the warrant and have done with it – but he defended this Jesus to the hilt, put himself on the line for him.

I suppose part of the reason was a thirst for justice. He might be a pig but he still has a slight streak of humanity and he really believed in this guy's innocence. I suspect the larger reason was stubbornness, though; once he'd declared the man's innocence it would take a furious force to budge him. As I said before, he's as stubborn as a mule.

* * *

(*Looks at hands and fingernails*) To be honest, I don't normally take any interest in his work. My days are busy enough as it is, with manicures, pedicures and follicle treatments, without having to concern myself with matters of state! But I did get interested in this case. Didn't have much choice – it was all he ever spoke about. And the pressure was mounting on him. All the chief priests and Jewish leaders, even the general public, were turning against this poor Jesus. But he was determined not to reverse his decision. Yes, he still wanted to save this carpenter, but he also wanted to save face, not show any sign of weakness. It takes a lot to make my husband break into a sweat, but that night he was worried – I mean, *really* worried.

The next morning he awoke early, and he had a plan of rescue. He would offer to release to the people a prisoner, either Jesus or this murderer they also had in the cells. I suppose he thought it would be a foregone conclusion.

I awoke a bit later from a terrible nightmare. A nightmare depicting the calamity which would befall us if he killed that man. A revelation that this Jesus was a good and honourable man – truly the Son of God, just as he had said. Quickly and fearfully I wrote a note. I can't remember exactly what I said, but it was to the effect of 'Leave that good man alone'. But of course, it was too late.

* * *

When they crucified him, I·watched the different reactions. At the cross the masses were cheering, while just a few close friends were crying. The chief priests and elders were smiling, pleased at a job well done, another threat silenced. And my husband, when he returned home – I saw an empti-ness, a man aware of his fatal weakness. And as I looked at him I couldn't help but think, 'He had his chance, his moment to stand up for what was right, but he let it by.'

I suppose we all have such moments, too. The question is, do we let them pass?

Bible reference: Matthew 27:19

CHRISTMAS

12. Travellers' Lodge

'Then there was a knock at the door. Well, I would have answered it myself, but I was in my nightie and I had my curlers in, so I let lummox answer it. Big mistake!'

WIFE

This time he's gone too far!

It's just like a typical man, isn't it? They never know when to stop. I should be used to it by now, with my hopeless lummox of a husband, but he never fails to amaze me.

Let me explain. We're in the innkeeping business, have been for the best part of 15 years, and a very successful little inn we run, too. It's called 'the Travellers' Lodge'. If things continue to go well we're hoping to expand into the regions of Nazareth and Gaza in the next couple of years. That's if my husband doesn't blow the whole operation beforehand.

At the moment it's census time, by far the busiest time for anyone in the innkeeping game. We've got people trudging in from all over the shop, and we've been fully booked for weeks, even months. Now, *officially* we're licensed by the health and safety department to lodge a maximum of 36 guests. *Unofficially* it goes up by about 20 at census and holiday times. To do this we house a few up on the roof, make up some beds down in the wine cellar, and we even shove a mattress in the cupboard under the stairs and advertise it as a compact double. Of course it's not strictly legit, but as long as we don't go too overboard we can just bung the health and safety officer a few denarii and he turns a blind eye. And that's exactly what my problem is with my dear husband – not knowing when to stop!

Last night, when we got into bed, we agreed the inn was full to capacity. There were 62 people on the register, and the place was quite simply packed to the rafters. No way, not under any circumstances, could we take in any more guests. We agreed, there and then!

Then there was a knock at the door. Well, I would have answered it myself, but I was in my nightie and I had my curlers in, so I let lummox answer it. Big mistake! He always was one for a sob story, and this was a sob story to end all sob stories.

* * *

At the door were a young couple. Apparently they looked absolutely shattered. He was stood up front, ready to drop, and she was as pregnant as they come, sat on top of this mangy-looking donkey. They couldn't find anywhere to stay, they were worn out, she was ready to drop her sprog – so could we find them a space?

Now, you might think me heartless, but if it was me down there, I would have politely told them that I was very sorry and sent them on their way. Sounds cruel, but there's only so much charity you can give. But not so with lummox!

Twenty minutes later he comes back into the bedroom to tell me the tale. Lovely young couple, very tired, she heavily pregnant, no other options, etc, etc. So he's taken them in and put them up – wait for it – in the stable – the stable! Well, I hit the roof, didn't I! 'We've got health and safety coming in tomorrow morning. There's only so much he'll turn a blind eye to. What happens if he checks in the stable and sees a young woman flat on her back giving birth amongst bails of damp straw and a load of cow dung?'

'I hadn't thought of that,' he says. Well, of course he hadn't! He hadn't thought about it, 'cos he doesn't think – ever!

* * *

The following morning I confess I was in a bit of a mood. I popped in to see the young couple with a spot of breakfast, and I admit they were a lovely looking pair. I tried to be polite – a necessity in my game – but I was probably a bit on the curt side, still worried about the health and safety visit.

In addition to that, the morning was fraught with activity. While I was serving all the guests their breakfasts, the young woman went into labour. My husband was chasing between the kitchen and the stable with towels and pails of hot water, looking like a man possessed! Serves him right.

And when the child was born, I went in to take a look. He

73

was a beautiful thing, and the parents appeared totally awe-struck. What a terrible way for a child to come into the world, I thought. Hopefully, as life goes on, things will get better for him.

But things didn't slow down then. First, a group of shepherds came to visit the new baby. Goodness only knows where they got their information. They squeezed into the stable and presented the parents with some cute baby lambs as a sign of respect. A while later there was a bit of a furore in the street outside, as three kingly looking gentlemen turned up riding on camels. They parked them outside and asked to visit the new-born king, so we ushered them into the stable too – well, by that stage I thought the more, the merrier!

But then came the crunch. A little after half past four the health and safety officer turned up. He checked round the rooms inside and seemed satisfied to let the overcrowding issue go – for the usual financial agreement, of course. But then he insisted on taking a look inside the stable, and try as I might I couldn't deter him.

To say he was shocked would be something of an under-statement! There in the stable a young mother was nursing her child, her husband lovingly looking on. There was a collection of gruff shepherds and wise-looking gentlemen full of eastern promise. Add to this every farmyard animal known to man and my lummox of a husband with a vacuum cleaner, and you have quite an interesting picture.

The officer turned to me in confusion, and I smiled, as if to say, 'Just an average day in your friendly Travellers' Lodge!' Then, just as I thought it might get nasty, one of the nice-looking gents opened up a box and passed the officer a large golden ring, studded with rubies and diamonds. After a short pause he smiled and declared that our inn met the requirements of the health and safety department. I'm sure my relief was apparent to all!

* * *

They've all gone now, the couple with their child and all the guests. The census will soon be over and things will get back to normal. But from now on, every time I go into that stable it'll make me think. Just for a moment, it'll make me think . . .

Bible reference: Luke 2:1–21

 **CHRISTMAS**

13. Carrots with Garlic Dip

'My back's never been right, not since my
headline-grabbing journey carrying
you-know-who . . .'

DONKEY

They've got me in this retirement home now. Mount Lodge, it's called. Not very original, is it? Mind you, I shouldn't complain – it's done up lovely. Beautiful stables – the decoration is impeccable. And three meals a day: carrot for breakfast, carrot for lunch and carrot for tea – not a great variety, but it's always fresh, I'll give them that. And I don't mean to gossip, but some of the other donkeys in here – well, to be honest, they've seen better days. One's got a missing eye, there's a couple with water on the knee, there's one with a wonky ear and another one who has got the worst case of halitosis I have ever encountered. It's enough to make you bray!

Still, all things considered, I suppose I've seen better days. My back's never been right, not since my headline-grabbing journey carrying you-know-who. And here at Mount Lodge I get respect for that. I'm the official top donkey, so to speak. No, when the new ones arrive it's only a matter of hours before I'm being pointed out by the others: 'Look, that one over there; that's the one that carried her all the way from Nazareth to Bethlehem.'

As if I needed any reminding, with a permanent curve in my spine.

* * *

Seems amazing though, that it all happened the best part of eight years ago. I'd been up for sale in this pet shop called 'Sylvia's Pet Emporium' for I don't know how long. And in all that time no one had even given me a sideways glance. Every time a potential customer was in the shop I tried my hardest to look cuddly and cute, but to be honest it's a bit tricky when you've got a set of gnashers like Janet Street-Porter! Then one day, out of the blue, in comes this chap, looking a bit harassed. He comes straight up to me, gives me a quick once-over, then declares I'm perfect – exactly what he is looking for. So he pays up and off I trot, new horizons sprawling before me. Or so I thought.

When we got home, it was obvious fairly quickly we were about to take a trip. There were bags packed all over the place and no obvious spot for me to take a much-deserved rest. And just when I thought things couldn't get any worse, *she* appeared: my new mistress. To describe her as 'pregnant' would be underplaying it: she looked fit to burst. And it soon became apparent that not only was I expected to carry all their worldly possessions, but her as well, bump included!

In the light of how things turned out I should be grateful for the privilege, but at the time I was seriously miffed! So would you have been. Do you know how far it is from Nazareth to Bethlehem? Well, I'll tell you – it's a flipping long way! Especially with that lot on your back. And the condition of the roads is terrible. I blame the Romans. None of your nice smooth tarmac – it was all bumpy and dusty. I was stumbling around all over the place, thinking my poor ankles would never be the same again. Every time I even slightly dipped my head I got an eyeful of grit and dust! Oh, it was the most miserable time of my life. I spent most of the time daydreaming about the good old days back at Sylvia's Pet Emporium.

Anyway, after travelling for goodness knows how long, we arrived in Bethlehem. The place was heaving with visitors, and of course his nibs, the Brain of Nazareth, hadn't booked us a room! I ask you! Even I know you have to advance-book accommodation, and I'm a donkey! Eventually some generous chap offers us his stable. Not particularly suitable for a pregnant woman, but for a shattered donkey it was perfect. As soon as we got in there I went to the corner and crashed out. Then I slept. And I slept like I've never slept before or since.

While I was sleeping, some amazing things happened, apparently. A huge star appeared over the stable, indicating the birth of a king. The child was born and there were

79

visitors from far and wide bringing greetings and gifts. Some visitors even arrived on camels. I was very happy to have missed *them*: camels smell even worse than halitosis-breath over there. But I missed it all, curled up in the corner in my coma-like sleep. Still, as my nanny always used to say, if you slept that long, you must have needed it!

When I finally awoke, I thought we might at least be spending a few days in Bethlehem, just to see some sights, but no such luck. The first thing I noticed was that all the bags were packed again, and there was even more stuff this time, what with all the baby gifts! The couple were clucking around, getting ready for the trip. I've no idea what all the rush was, but the destination, I overheard, was to be Egypt. Imagine it: Nazareth to Egypt – my poor ankles! And it was an eventful trip, full of excitement and intrigue – but I'll save that one for another day.

* * *

Ooh, look at the time! Just about ready for supper, I think. And what's on today's menu, I wonder? Looks like carrots with a garlic dip – my favourite! I tell you, there's nothing like the life of a donkey.

Bible reference: Matthew 2:13–15

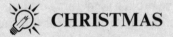 **CHRISTMAS**

14. Extraordinary News

'"A sword will pierce your own soul, too." As he
said this he looked at me, and there were tears in
his eyes.'

MARY

Kids! Who'd have 'em!

I suppose at one time or another all mothers have uttered those immortal words – but few, I'm sure, have ever really meant it! Even my own mother has said it a few times, usually when I've broken something or gone into a mood for some insignificant reason. But never did she come closer to meaning it than on the day I told her my extraordinary news. I mean, I've always wanted kids, ever since I can first remember playing with dolls, but even so, I wasn't planning on having one quite so soon . . .

Why would I? What's the big rush? Life was really good. I had a strong faith, a wonderful family, and a new fiancé – a gorgeous local carpenter by the name of Joseph. Things were so good I would walk around with a permanent grin on my face. But things were about to get better, unbelievably better, but in a rather strange way.

One day, out of the blue, no appointment or anything, this angel appears. I know it sounds a bit far-fetched, but that's how it happened – no word of a lie! And this angel says to me that I'm pregnant, that I'm carrying God's own Son – the promised Messiah – and that I should name him Jesus.

However unbelievable the story sounds, the most unbelievable thing is that not for one second did I doubt its authenticity. I don't want to sound super-spiritual – I'm as human as the next person, with faults and foibles – but I knew, without a shadow of a doubt I knew. I asked how it was physically possible, which was explained, and then I said, 'I am the Lord's servant, and I am willing to do whatever he wants. May everything you said come true.' And I meant it.

After the initial adrenalin rush died down, it dawned on me that the job of explaining the situation might be easier said than done. My parents were shocked – there's no escaping it. They said they believed me. Of course they would – they loved me dearly – but I could detect in their eyes a flicker of doubt. A fear of madness, maybe? I went to see my Aunt Elizabeth, who was also pregnant, and as soon as she caught sight of me she greeted me, 'Mother of my Lord!' I don't know how she knew, but I was grateful she did.

And then of course there was dear Joseph. Confused and fearful, he so wanted to believe. And if there was one person I needed to understand it was him. Thankfully, the angel had the foresight to pay him a visit too, and I knew that with him standing by my side I could weather any storm – the storms of my peers and townsfolk with their disapproving looks and sly comments, the storms of physical pain and exhaustion which accompanied the often-told circumstances of the birth. But Joseph was there, always there, every step of the way.

I won't bore you with all the details of the birth – it's been reported in just about every tabloid journal in the East. But I will tell you something they don't repeat.

After eight days we took our child to the Temple in Jerusalem in order to present him to God, as was our custom. There we named him Jesus and offered a sacrifice of two young pigeons and a pair of doves. In the Temple courts we were met by an old man. Taking our son into his arms, he said, 'My eyes have seen your salvation.' Joseph and I were moved to tears as he spoke these words over our Jesus. But then, among other things, he said, 'A sword will pierce your own soul, too.' As he said this he looked at me, and there were tears in his eyes. 'A sword will pierce your own soul, too.'

* * *

Later, after we had completed everything required by the law, we returned to Galilee, to our home town of Nazareth. And here we remain. Jesus is 14 now and has gained quite some reputation. He has incredible wisdom, far beyond his years, although I know all mothers say that. And he has grown strong. He's his father's apprentice – my two carpenters –

though secretly Joseph and I know he's destined for other, greater things.

* * *

Sometimes, when I'm on my own, I allow my thoughts to wander. And I think of that old man back in Jerusalem and recall his words: 'A sword will pierce your own soul, too.' And I fear what they might mean. Still, I suppose this is the pain and privilege of motherhood.

Kids! Who'd have them? I would. Every time, from the bottom of my heart, I would.

Bible references: Luke 1:38; 2:34

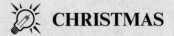 **CHRISTMAS**

15. An Unforgettable Christmas

'We talk about the old times, the mistakes, the
lessons. We begin to build a future together,
without loneliness, only happiness.'

Props

Armchair	Watch	*Sound*
Glass	TV guide	Doorbell
Pot Noodle	Books	'Unforgettable',
Fork	Phone	Nat King Cole
Bottle of vodka	10 Xmas cards	Buzzer
Cheese footballs	Box for cards	Phone ring
Bowl of nuts	Xmas cracker	National anthem
Nutcrackers	Photo of Kate	
Cassette player	Photo album	
Papers and magazine		

(*As the lights go up we hear the end of the national anthem.*
JOHN *is sitting asleep on his armchair. He is holding an empty
glass and there is a Pot Noodle on his lap. The final bars of the
anthem wake him up.*)

JOHN

Oh no! That's three straight years I've done that – missed the
Queen's speech . . . (*He moves in his chair and the Pot Noodle
falls. It has solidified in the pot and the fork is stuck. He pours
a large drink.*)

I never used to miss it. Part of the perfect Christmas. Open
the pressies in the morning, have a slap-up Christmas lunch,
watch the Queen's speech, then doze off during *Chitty Chitty
Bang Bang*. I know they show her again at teatime, but it's
not the same, is it? That's like watching the repeat. At three
o'clock it's live . . . Well, obviously it's not actually live 'cos
it's on the radio earlier. In fact it's recorded days, weeks,
before Christmas. I bet you didn't know that! (*He plays
around with a variety of snacks by the side of his chair. Eats a
cheese football, grimaces, then spits it out.*)

UGGGHHH!! Why do we buy cheese footballs at
Christmas? They taste like vomit. (*Starts throwing them at*

bin.) Not bad for target practice, though! What we buy, really! Dates. It's ridiculous. Brandy snaps, twiglets, those diagonal cheese savouries, baskets full of nuts. No wonder Christmas is so flipping expensive. Now nuts, I must admit they are a bit different. (*He goes to table where there is a bowl of nuts.*) A lot of hassle, but very nice. Monkey nuts are my favourite, mainly 'cos I never quite got the hang of the nut-crackers. (*Eats nuts and starts choking. Takes a swig of vodka straight from the bottle to stop it.*)

That'll do the trick. Now, where's the TV guide? (*Hunts through a pile of papers and magazines.*) Ah, here we are. AGGHHH! Noel Edmonds! (*Acts vomiting.*) Now, what classic movies have we got on today? Ah, here we are . . . (*Starts singing.*) 'The hills are alive with the sound of music ah ah ah agghhhh' . . . (*Song trails off into noise of strangulation.*) Every year, it drives you mad. I've never actually stayed awake for the duration of that one. I'd have to be pumped with a few shots of adrenalin first. (*Sings James Bond theme, ding dinga ling ling etc.*) That's more like it. I mean, what would Christmas and Bank Holidays be like without a good old Bond movie? Now, which one is it? *Thunderball*! Good – a Sean Connery one. So, *Thunderball* it is. That's on at 5.55. Now, if I can just get through the next two-and-a-half hours . . . (*He wanders around looking at books, checking phone is on hook and starts looking at Christmas cards.*)

* * *

You might think that for a sad old loner I've got quite a number of cards, but I suppose I ought to come clean on this one. You see, about a week ago I only had four cards. My sister in Australia – now hers came in early November 'cos she likes to make sure it's not late. Mum and Dad's. Rob, my university pal who's currently doing a panto in Morecambe – and this is the best one, I think you'll be quite impressed –

Tony and Cherie Blair. Surprised? Well, don't get too excited. Apparently the Labour party have targeted my postal code prefix for a pre-election push. Still. It's a nice thought . . . creeps! So there they are, the sacred four.

Now, I said to myself, if I get one more a day until Christmas Eve that'll be ten – double figures, that's socially acceptable. But since Jeffrey Archer's got more chance of becoming Prime Minister than I have of getting ten Christmas cards, I decided to cheat and get out last year's. Well, the last three years', actually. I keep them in a box in case of an emergency. (*Produces a box.*) I mean, if I had a guest on, say, December 23rd, and I only had four cards, they would be immediately put off. However, as it is now, a guest would be highly impressed. 'Goodness me, John,' they would exclaim. 'You must have a very wide circle of friends.'

Nobody did visit on the 23rd, or any other day come to that, but you just don't know. You could get a visitor any time . . . (*He closes his eyes. Doorbell rings once . . . twice . . . long single ring.*)

That doorbell you might have heard, it's not actually my doorbell. It's actually my imagination. I often hear my bell ring. I imagine answering the door to all manner of interesting people. Actors, politicians, vets, computer engineers, library assistants . . . I invite them in, we talk, laugh, drink. (*Pours a large drink. Bell rings.*) 'But how do you know it's not really your bell?' I hear you say. Because my bell is broken, and anyway I know, because even when it worked it never rang. Never rang.

* * *

What was I saying? Ah, the cards . . . Yes, so out came last year's, two years ago and three years ago. Now three years ago I was still at the office. It was a few months before I had become 'surplus to requirements'! 'I'm very sorry, Mr Sharpe. Believe me, your twelve years' long, hard service makes this job even harder than it already is, but what with the economy as it stands, the old firm is feeling the pinch and the advertising and marketing department, like the others, has to suffer. I'm sure you understand.' So, hence the box of cards from my old work pals. It's worked out very handy to have them now. (*Pulls cracker with himself, puts on hat, tells joke and plays with gift.*)

Since I left the old firm things have been a bit thin on the cards front. Bit thin on the everything front – friends, visitors, going out, hair! I haven't really got anything to show from before three years ago, before Kate and I split. Well, before Kate walked out. Twenty-first of October 1997, at approximately quarter past six. I thought everything was fine, but I hadn't reckoned on Alasdair. (*Blows raspberry.*) Alasdair, the hunky chunky surveyor from East Dulwich. Swept her off her feet. Twelve years together gone. Pooff . . . a mere trifle. I put a manly face on it. (*Mimics a cool dude:*) 'Yeah, babe, you're probably right, time to move on. You know what they say: if you love someone, set them free. If they come back again, then in the end it was meant to be.'

But I didn't want to let her go free. I wanted her exclusively for myself. I wanted to give myself exclusively to her, no one else. It wasn't selfish, it was absolute love – bordering on obsession. We were never apart. Here's her picture. And oh, I'll play you our song – it's an absolute classic. (*Finds tape, then plays Nat King Cole's, 'Unforgettable'. He looks through photo album, singing along. Pours large drink.*)

We didn't keep any Christmas cards in the years we were together. We used to cut out the pictures with pinking shears and donate them to Save the Dolphins to sell the following year as gift tags. I mean, why need to feel popular and loved by friends when we had each other? It was complete, perfect, unforgettable. (*Picks up nutcrackers.*) 'Hello, Alasdair, it's lovely to meet you.' (*Throws down crackers.*) Oh, when is that Bond movie going to start? Two hours and eleven minutes precisely.

Have you ever tried a Christmas on your own? Oh, they are unforgettable. It's funny how Christmas is a kind of magnifier of how you feel. If you're a happy family it makes you happier; if you're sad it gets you really sad; if you're generous you have a huge spend; if you're tight it makes you feel mega-stingy. And if you're lonely, well, you can guess. How can I explain it? Everything about Christmas, the TV shows, the gifts, the colours, the decorations, the happy songs, the cards, they all seem to scream out, 'You are sad and lonely!' When it's not Christmas it's bearable.

Christ born in a stable of a virgin – was it to save me or torment me?

Ah well, I suppose it's my own fault. I didn't have to be on my own. I mean, the phone is two-way. I could have gone with Mum and Dad over to their friends, the Butlers. There's always a big crowd there. They would have welcomed me, but they're all so flipping happy. I was going to phone Mum about going this year but, I don't know, a 37-year-old man going to a Christmas do with his mum and dad. Saddo! I mean, it's not pride. Well, yeah, I suppose it is pride, really.

I could have gone to see Rob in Morecambe. I nearly picked up the phone for that one. 'Hey, Rob, how about a visitor for Christmas?' 'Yeah, great, mate! Any time – it gets boring up here between shows. We could hit some bars, find some fillies, eh! I'll flash my Equity card about, let them all know I'm an actor – they'll be falling at our feet!' It could have been good fun, I admit, but they're doing three shows a day, for goodness' sake. By the time he's got out of his camel's rear-end costume we'll only have half an hour before he's back on again. And the accommodation – well, you think this is bad? A flea-infested damp dump in a Morecambe guest house with the Wicked Witch of the West as your landlady is not my ideal digs. No, give me *Mary Poppins* and a Pot Noodle any day.

*   *   *

I suppose that brings me back to Kate. I don't think I told you the rest of the Alasdair saga. You're probably thinking to yourself, while I sit here alone, Kate and Alasdair are by contrast having a happy family Christmas with their 2.4 children and two-thirds of a dog. (*Buzzer noise.*) Wrong! They didn't have a happy ending. No, after a year Alasdair the stud gave Kate a taste of her own medicine. He left her for a younger, more attractive model. I don't know if he's still with her – probably changed a couple of times since. Blokes like him always do. But Kate, Kate's on her own. I hear she lives alone in a flat in Hove, depressed and lonely. Similar to me, really, except she's more a *Sound of Music* kinda girl! I know what you're all thinking: call her up. I've thought about it. Believe me, every day I think about it, but if she wants me, she can get in touch. I'm ready – I think I'm ready. (*The phone rings;* JOHN *ignores it.*)

*   *   *

That phone you might have heard, it's not actually my phone. It's actually my imagination. I often hear it ring. I imagine answering it to all manner of interesting people – to Kate. We talk about the old times, the mistakes, the lessons. We begin to build a future together, without loneliness, only happiness. (*Phone rings again.*) 'But how do you know it's not your phone ringing?' I hear you say. Because my phone is broken. (*He picks up phone and we can see it is disconnected.*) And I know anyway, because even when it worked, it never rang. (*He throws the phone down and pours another drink.*)

I have built the ultimate defence mechanism for my emotions. No one visits, no one calls. I visit no one, I call no one. Let nobody near you. Protect your territory, then nobody can hurt you. A life without hurt – it's as easy as that. But the price is high. Nobody can hurt you, but nobody can love

91

you. That's the deal. Did you know that statistics show that the suicide rate at Christmas increases? I wonder why.

Oh, don't panic – I've done this before on numerous occasions. But what have I got to live for? A James Bond film and a leftover chicken sandwich? (*He sings 'Unforgettable' to himself and starts crying.*) Kate . . . (*'Unforgettable' plays as lights fade to blackout.*)

Bible reference: Proverbs 18:24

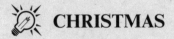 **CHRISTMAS**

16. Christmas in Our House

'Why do they 'ave to go so overboard on religion
at Christmas? It's got nothing to do with
Christmas. Not in our house, anyway!'

Introduction

This piece can either be read as a rhyme or acted out as a monologue. Either way, it should be performed using a 'common as muck' character voice, with lots of energy.

MAN

Why do they 'ave to go so overboard on religion at
    Christmas?
It's got nothing to do with Christmas. Not in our house,
    anyway!
In our house Christmas is about food and booze!

An excessive plethora of gorging and devouring, boozing
    and bingeing, gulping and swilling.
Sixteen-pound turkeys, stuffed with Mr Paxo's sage and
    onion deluxe,
Two-foot-wide craters abundantly overflowing with nuts.

Novelty biscuits shaped like Wallace and Gromit,
Little cheese footballs that smell like vomit.

We pop open a tube of Pringles, then enter the Twiglet
    zone,
Spread out a cold meat buffet, but avoid beef on the bone!

A ten-pound tin of Roses we continuously nosh,
Or a tray of Ferrero Rocher, if we're feeling rather posh.

Lumps of cheese and pineapple, impaled on wooden sticks,
Christmas pud and brandy butter – now I'm feeling very
    sick!
The mother-in-law shouts over, 'You're a revolting, mon-
    strous lout!'
I says to her, 'Mind yer business, and finish off yer sprouts!'

My belt is getting rather tight, I'm ready to flaming burst,
Time for an alcoholic bender, to quench my rampant
  thirst.

Start with a crate of lagers, from the beano to France on
  the ferry,
Then some wine and vodka, with a generous dash of
  sherry.

I offer the mother-in-law a whisky, 'Ooh, I don't know if I
  dare!'
Then she coyly takes the bottle, and drains it till it's bare!

The wife has just fallen down the stairs, she's totally out of
  her tree,
I warned her to take it easy with that Bailey's Irish Cream.

Empty bottles, cans and wrappers, all adorn our living-
  room floor,
Then some cheeky little carol singers come knocking on
  the door.

'Away in a manger, no crib for a bed.
The little Lord Jesus lays down his sweet head.'

Why do they 'ave to go so overboard on religion at
  Christmas?
It's got nothing to do with Christmas. Not in our house,
  anyway!
In our house Christmas is all about pressies and televisual
  feasts.

Enormous hoards and masses of totally useless gifts,
Rarely anything you actually want, which always gets me
  miffed.

Packs of initialled hankies from Aunt Dot and Uncle Malc,
Santa socks and boxer shorts, and a dozen tubes of talc.

Writing things and bathroom things and loads of worthless
   junk,
Bottles of cheap, old eau de cologne that leave you smell-
   ing like a skunk.

I got the missus a Michael Ball CD, singing songs from all
   the shows,
And a set of naughty undies, which when it's dark begin to
   glow!

There's enough wrapping paper kicking round to rob a rain
   forest of all its trees,
But at least the pressies are out the way, now we can con-
   centrate on TV.

Cilla Black's *Surprise Surprise* always makes us cry,
The Sound of Music, *Mary Poppins*, *Bridge on the River
   Kwai*.

Supercudgafudgealisticexpialidocious,
I've never sat all through that film, it's so totally atrocious.

Top of the Pops at lunch time is an interminable drone –
When I say that Will and Gareth are naff, the kids both
   start to moan.

The Christmas specials are out in force, one after another,
Only Fools and Horses, then that one *Birds of a Fuvver*!

Rolf Harris is blubbing on *Animal Hospital*, the daft
   Australian eejit.
And *One Foot in the Grave* with Victor screaming, 'I don't
   believe it!'

Two fun-packed hours of *EastEnders* and their miserable
family rifts,
The *Songs of Praise* extravaganza, with special guest star
Cliff.

Jim Davidson's Generation Game is on in just a trice.
He's not as good as Brucey was – 'Nice to see you, to see
you, nice!'

Of course the Queen's Speech at three is a total and absolute must.
She's a devoted, wonderful woman, and in God she truly
trusts.

So food and booze and pressies and telly are the order of
the day.
It all seems rather empty, but who can really say?

I still don't know why they go so overboard on religion at
Christmas.
Stars and stables, wise men and angels, all appear a tad
obsessive.

Perhaps one day an exciting, different meaning will shake
me from my rut,
But just for now I'm going to bed – well, maybe just a few
more nuts!

 **CHRISTMAS**

17. Blood and Tinsel

'Somewhere amongst all the blood and tinsel, I
think I've lost the true meaning of Christmas.'

(*MAN comes charging in, looking suitably distressed.*)

MAN

So the whole thing is a disaster! A complete, epoch-making, monumental disaster! I mean, I'm not asking for much, am I? Christmas is supposed to be a time of festive cheer and 'joy to the world', isn't it? Well, isn't it!?

Caroline, my beloved wife, is currently refusing to speak to me. All intimacy, civility and verbal communications are suspended indefinitely.

And the reason for this devastating state of affairs? Trying to decide which set of parents to spend Christmas Day with! Pathetic, isn't it? To be honest with you, I couldn't give two hoots where I am – leave me here with a four-pack and a James Bond movie and I'll be deliriously happy. It's just everyone else that has to be so flipping difficult!

* * *

It all started a few weeks back when Caroline says to me, 'Ooh Dave, about the Christmas arrangements: I thought we'd go over to my mum and dad's for Christmas Day, then yours on Boxing Day for your mum's famous cold meat buffet.'

'Fine,' I say. 'Whatever.' But when I spoke to my mum later that evening the news was given a somewhat frosty reception.

'Mum,' I say. 'For Christmas we're planning to go to Caroline's parents for Christmas Day, then over to you for Boxing Day and the famous cold meat buffet. Is that okay with you?'

'It'll have to be, won't it!?' she says.

'Woh, woh, woh,' I say. 'What's up with you? I don't understand.'

'Well, you wouldn't. Typical man! It's just you always go to Caroline's parents for Christmas Day and sideline us onto

100

Boxing Day. I know we haven't got all them posh mod cons like they have, but it would be nice, just one year, to see my only grandson on Christmas Day.'

'But what about your famous Boxing Day cold meat buffet?' I says.

'I only do that to try and give Boxing Day a bit more excitement. When you're used to being treated as second best, you just have to try and make the most of it, don't you?'

'Well, if you feel that strongly about it, of course we'll come to you on Christmas Day.'

'I don't want to be a burden.'

'*You're not being a burden!* I'm sure it will be perfectly fine to switch.'

How wrong could I have been . . .

* * *

I approached Caroline with my new plan.

'Mum's feeling a bit sidelined,' I says. 'I thought we could switch this year and see my parents on Christmas Day and yours on Boxing Day. It would make her feel much better.'

'Well what about my poor parents?' says Caroline. 'I suppose it's all right to sideline them just to appease your mum's amateur dramatics.'

'Hang on,' says I. 'Hang on! We always see your parents on Christmas Day. It won't harm to switch for one year.'

'Ah, but that's only because your mum always does her disgusting cold meat buffet on Boxing Day.'

'Yes, but she only does the famous cold meat buffet to make the most of us treating her like a second-class citizen.'

At this point Caroline starts to cry.

'You've always hated my parents, haven't you? Ever since you first met them.'

'Au contraire,' I says, 'au contraire. I've always found them very . . . well, very *pleasant*.' Bad choice of word, I admit.

'Pleasant! May I remind you they gave us £4,000 for the

deposit on this house. Without them we could never have managed. And what did your parents give us? A bit of fluffy carpet to stick on the toilet lid and a set of non-stick saucepans!'

'Don't knock them saucepans,' I says. 'They came with a lifetime guarantee!'

More crying.

At this point, Harry, my wonderful teenage son, entered into the proceedings. Caroline, latching onto a piece of potential leverage, tried her hand at a bit of manipulation.

'Harry, given the choice of a fun-packed Christmas at Nanny and Grandad's or a lousy buffet at Grandma and Grandpa B's, which would you prefer?'

Harry briefly paused, and then hit her with his teenage wisdom.

'Neither. They're all totally boring and their houses stink of mothballs.'

Needless to say, this once again sent Caroline into mild hysteria! She stormed upstairs and I was left to berate Harry for his tactless – albeit accurate – observations about our parents' slightly rancid homes.

* * *

So, where does that leave us, I hear you ask. Well, I'll tell you.

Are we spending Christmas Day at my parents'? No.

Are we spending it at Caroline's parents'? No.

Both sets of parents sensed a boiling-point atmosphere and so withdrew their kind invitations, neither wishing to prove a burden. Leaving the three of us here, alone – me, with my four-pack of stout and *Mary Poppins* on the telly, Caroline sulking in the bedroom with the latest Jackie Collins and a bottle of advocaat, and Harry in his room, on his new Xbox.

And you know, I got to thinking: this isn't what Christmas used to be like. I can recall all the fun, the carols, the excite-

ment, the warm love, the Morecambe and Wise special . . .
but it's all disappeared.

I don't know. Somewhere amongst all the blood and
tinsel, I think I've lost the true meaning of Christmas.

(*We hear a group of carol singers.*)

Can you hear that? Carol singers! Where's that bucket of
water?

Bible reference: Proverbs 15:1

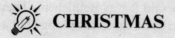 **CHRISTMAS**

18. Paparazzi!

'I cradled him in my arms and I felt a real
warmth – he'd wet himself down the front of my
brand new Yves St Laurent shirt!'

CHRIS

(*To himself*) All the way from the city I came to cover this story.

'Go on, Christopher,' they said. 'It's a royal birth, a once-in-a-lifetime opportunity.' I might've known something was fishy when they said it was Bethlehem. They must think my aftershave is eau de dung, all the ploppy old jobs they give me.

* * *

(*Notices audience.*) Oh, do excuse me. Please allow me to introduce myself, ladies and gentlemen: Christopher St John[1] Smythe's the name, freelance photographer for the *Judea Chronicle*. Also available for weddings, graduations and the odd glamour shoot – reasonable rates, of course. Currently residing in the entertainment capital of Eastern civilisation – Bethlehem! Why Bethlehem, I hear you ask? And well you may. To cover a royal birth. And I can tell you, it's been a real eye-opener from the beginning.

When I first arrived in town, I thought I'd check into a posh hotel – you know, the ones with monogrammed towels and duck-feather pillows. Wrong! No one in Bethlehem had even heard of a hotel, much less owned one. One of the townsfolk informed me, 'You'll 'ave to find an inn, but they're prob'ly all filled up 'cos of the census.' Well, can you imagine, me, Christopher St John Smythe, residing in an inn?! A joke. Still, with so few options I eventually found one owned by a snaggle-toothed old hag who agreed to take me in. 'Oh yes, my dear, I'll squeeze you in. I always feel a bit sorry for you bald, ugly ones.' I was left with little or no choice.

So, after I'd settled into my cupboard under the stairs, I decided to venture out into Bethlehem to find the royal palace. I was expecting a welcoming committee for the

---

[1] St John pronounced 'sinjun'

world's press, with a generous spread of champagne and prawn vindaloo vol-au-vents. How wrong could I have been! I was to find that Bethlehem has no royal palaces, no royalty, not even a duke! Just lots and lots of inns . . . and smelly stables. No, I wasn't to find myself surrounded by kingly robes, walking on polished marble floors in a royal palace, but instead I was stuck with a selection of the most revolting farmyard animals, knee-deep in animal poo in a ramshackle stable. Still, it was a lesson in humility, I suppose!

* * *

The alleged 'royal birth' was an interesting departure from what I had expected. The parents proudly looked down on their baby, and I must admit they did have an endearing, innocent charm about them. Mary and Joseph invited me into the stable, along with some shepherds, who had very originally brought gifts of sheep . . . They were full of some extraordinary story about angelic choirs giving a concert on the hillside or something. Haven't got time to check out their story. They seemed genuine enough but, of course, simple country folk like that can be very gullible.

Mary smiled at me and asked if I would like to hold the child. I did. I cradled him in my arms and I felt a real warmth – he'd wet himself down the front of my brand new Yves St Laurent shirt! As I laid the baby back in the manger, our eyes met, and I had the distinct feeling that this was no ordinary baby. I felt he had great insight and would grow up to be a remarkable young man.

* * *

I suppose, unfortunately, a child born in a stable is just another sign of the times. Personally I blame New Labour. Don't suppose any of this will be remembered in five or ten years' time, will it? Yet somehow I feel good about myself, uplifted. Call me sentimental, but this poor, young family has really touched me. I'm not a religious man, although I do believe in God of course, but holding that baby was the nearest thing to a spiritual experience I can remember – almost as though God was trying to get a message through to me . . .

Anyway, enough of all this – must dash. Just had some hot gossip that some celebrity stargazers are heading for Herod's palace. Could be a great photo story, so I'm off to get the exclusive!

Bible reference: Luke 2:8–20

 **CHRISTMAS**

19. Joseph's Bethlehem Experience

'I must confess, I did find her story regarding the
father's identity a little bit on the far-fetched side.'

JOSEPH

I'm happy, very happy. Incredibly happy! But it wasn't always this way. No. A couple of thousand years ago it was a very different story. I mean, how would you feel? Picture the scene: I'd had a busy day at the carpentry workshop, knocking up a few bookcases, a wardrobe and a couple of mangers. I comes home for my tea, and the fiancée calls round and tells me she's with child. 'Joseph, darling, I've got something to tell you.' Not an everyday occurrence, it has to be said!

Now, I admit I was fairly naïve back then when it came to the old facts of life, but even I knew that holding hands and kissing on a regular basis didn't make a woman pregnant. An explanation was requested, in the nicest possible way, and duly given.

Now, I love my Mary more than anyone, so I immediately thought about how to save her from public disgrace and possible stoning. But I must confess, I did find her story regarding the father's identity a little bit on the far-fetched side. You probably would have yourself. I mean, I know all about the birds and the bees, but all this stuff Mary spun me about angels and heavenly hosts, and her having conceived by the Holy Spirit . . . Please! I thought she'd been on some other kind of spirit, if you catch my drift! (*Mimes swigging from a bottle.*)

* * *

Forgive me if, looking back on it now, I seem rather flippant. At the time, I was in the depths of despair. I mean, my Mary, my innocent virgin Mary, was pregnant. I feel guilty for thinking some of the things I thought, but come on, with the information available at the time, what would you have thought?

The history books of your ancestors look on me as somewhat insignificant, sort of in the background, only worth a few verses in the Bible. And I don't mind. I'm not looking for stardom. It would be nice to have a famous actor play me in a film, though. I'm always played by some unknown! Anyway, what people fail to see is that, at this stage, I was looking at Mary's pregnancy in purely human terms. I knew I hadn't touched her, so the only other possible explanation was Mary had been with another man, and that cut me up bad. It wasn't until I went to bed in a state of shock, to sleep on this revelation, that things took on a more spiritual level.

Now, I don't know if any of you have ever been visited by an angel. Well, it was my first time. 'Do not be afraid,' he said. 'Take Mary home as your wife. What she has conceived is of the Holy Spirit. Your son will save the people from their sins.' Mind-blowing stuff, eh! But my first feeling, when all this had sunk in, was relief. Pure relief that my Mary was telling the truth, innocence intact. Then it was total joy at the great privilege given to us, to bring God's own Son into this world. Amazing!

* * *

So, if you ever find your feelings go up and down a bit, remember the story of Joseph's emotional rollercoaster, from despair to relief and joy in one fell swoop! The Bethlehem experience has been life-changing for me. I hope it is for you. Don't let it pass you by as 'just a nice story'. Believe me, there's a lot more to it than that.

I was upset about one thing, though. I had hoped to call our first child something in the more modern line: Damon or Farquhar. But under the circumstances, we were happy to do what the prophets had foretold. So, in our makeshift maternity ward, all those years ago, we named our first son Jesus . . .

Bible reference: Matthew 1:18–25

111

SEVEN STAGES OF MAN

20. Part One: 'Oo's a clever boy, din!'

'Okay, I admit I can't speak yet, but that doesn't
make me a complete idiot, does it?'

Props

Costume   *Sound*

Large nappy   'You must have been a beautiful baby'
Bonnet   Recorded dialogue
Rattle

Introduction

*This series of seven linked monologues can be performed sep-
arately or all together. Based on Shakespeare's 'seven ages of
man' speech from* As You Like It, *it opens up seven windows
on the life of a character, Vince, taking him from newborn baby
to extreme old age.*

*They will be best performed as part of some teaching on the
meaning of life or 'where are we all going?' You will notice in
the scripts that often more than one character is used. These
parts are offstage voices, best done with a pre-recorded tape.
So the pieces all remain monologues, with just one performer
on stage.*

*They should all be performed with a strong, humorous cari-
cature style.*

(*Musical introduction relating to babies, eg 'You must have
been a beautiful baby'.* VINCE *enters in a baby outfit: large
nappy, bonnet and rattle. A tape-recording provides Grandma's
voice, which is responded to by* VINCE *with a collection of
appropriate baby noises.*)

GRANDMA

Hello! Hello!
   Oo's a lovely little boy, din?
   Oo's a lovely ickle boy, din?
   Can you say hello to Grandma? Can you say hello to
Grandma?

Say Grandma . . . (*Gaaa!*)

Oo's a clever boy! Grandma . . . (*Gaa!*)

Grandma . . . (*Gaa!*)

Grandma . . . (*Gangan*)

Grandma . . . (*Gangan*)

Oo's a clever boy! Let's find Mummy and show her. Shall Grandma find Mummy?

Shall Grandma find Mummy? . . . (*GAAAA!!*)

Don't worry, I'll be back in a minute. Grandma be back in a minute . . .

VINCE

(*Excited baby face suddenly becomes adult and cynical*) Oh well, whoopee-do, I can't wait!

I mean, has the woman got no shame, or is she just totally deranged!? Okay, I admit I can't speak yet, but that doesn't make me a complete idiot, does it? Of course I can't speak – I'm only six months old, for goodness' sake. I can't create meaningful syllables – my soft palate hasn't formed properly yet – so sue me! Anyway, it's lucky for dear Grandma it hasn't, 'cos if it had, the first thing I'd do is tell her to get out of my face! Well, her gnarled old fingers poking and prodding me, and her rancid old breath just about knocking me out; it's more than a young innocent such as I can bear.

* * *

So this is where my story begins. After nine months of luxurious hibernation, out I popped, greeted by my dear mother squealing her head off, drenched in sweat and, to be honest, not looking her best. My father was out cold on the floor, lying in a pool of afterbirth. And then a sadistic doctor, who took obvious pleasure in chopping off one of my finest appendages, was holding me upside down and whacking me on the bum! I tell you, if it had been physically possible to crawl back into the warmth of my mother's womb I would

115

have done so immediately, but by the look on the poor dear's face I thought she'd been through enough of an ordeal for one day. So here I remain, in the first stages of life, apparently fit only for mewling and puking in the nurse's arms.

Hang on – where's that dummy? (*VINCE has a quick suck on his dummy.*) That's better! Well, I certainly do my fair share of mewling. (*Loud, short blast of frenetic screaming.*) Not bad, eh? It amazes me when you hear people say, 'What's he crying about?' or 'Why do babies cry so much?' I mean, let's face it, there's not a lot else to do, is there? You can't move anywhere: you're stuck wherever you're dumped, like it or not. And if you try and move your head, even an inch, it spins round and round until you're sick with giddiness!

And my parents, love them as I do, will enjoy playing their funny little games. The other day they propped me up on the sofa and took bets on which direction I'd slump first, left or right. That kept them amused for hours. In wild hysterics, they were. Call me a killjoy, but personally I couldn't see the joke. And as for puking, well why not? Better out than in, so they say!

I don't mean to boast, but I have become a bit of a champ. I caught Grandma the other day with an awesome projectile vomit – must have been a good, oooh, four feet. All down her peach Marks and Spencer's twin set. She pretended it didn't matter: 'Oh, don't worry, it'll come out in the wash.' But I could tell underneath she was absolutely livid!

And my dad – I've clicked what his favourite top is too: this navy blue Adidas tracksuit thing. Whenever he's got it on, which is most of the time, he's not too keen on giving me a cuddle after feeding. So I've got my system. I cry and scream and wail until he finally gives in and picks me up, then I let one go all down his back – splat! 'Oh no, not again, love. It's every flaming time!' He's got this permanent stripy stain down it now. I don't think there's a washing powder known to medical science that can remove it.

It's petty, I know, and it does sometimes prick at my conscience a bit, but it passes the time of day, dunnit! And there's always someone to jump to the defence of a poor, helpless little baby – 'Oh, bless him. Oo didn't know what oo was doing, did oo?' Hmm, don't believe a word of it – know what I mean?

Oh no, she's coming back again! And what is that pink, rattly thing she's about to shove in my face? Oh, this really is all beneath me. Still, here goes. I suppose I'd better show willing. (*VINCE returns to baby gestures.*)

* * *

GRANDMA

Look who's back! Look who back, din!

It's Grandma . . . (*GaaGaa*)

Yes! Grandma! . . . (*GaaGaa*)

And she got a rattle.

A little rattle.

A lovely little rattle.

What does Vincey think of the rattle, din? (*VINCE blows a long and loud raspberry.*)

Oh! Oo's a clever little boy, din!

(*Music plays to fade.*)

 **SEVEN STAGES OF MAN**

21. Part Two: Gangan's Little Angel

'I'm not seven. I'm seven and a half. Nearly seven
and three-quarters, actually . . .'

Props

Costume	*Sound*
Cap	Recorded dialogue
School tie	
Shorts	
White shirt	
Satchel	

(*Musical intro relating to young children, eg 'Two little boys'.* VINCE *enters as a young boy with cap, shorts and a satchel.*)

VINCE

I went shopping the other day with my mummy. It was in ADSDA's. When we was in there we bumped into one of my mum's bestest friends, called Auntie Sharon. She was wearing these really tight red leggings, which were horrible 'cos they made her bottom look like a big raspberry jelly! (VINCE *demonstrates the wobble.*) And she said really annoying and stupid things like most adults do, like 'Hello little Vincey. You're growing up, aren't you!'

'Uuhhhh! No, I'm getting smaller, actually.' I only said that to myself inside my head, though. If I'd said it out loud my mummy would have probably hit me really hard on my bottom.

Then she said to my mummy, 'How old is little Vincey now?' And my mum said seven. *Seven! Uuhhhh!* I'm not seven. I'm seven and a half. Nearly seven and three-quarters, actually. I didn't say that out loud, neither. No, I just stood there looking up at them both like a little angel. (VINCE *pulls angelic pose.*) 'Cos that's what my grandma says I am – Gangan's little angel.

* * *

The reason I was in ADSDA's with Mummy, and not in school, was 'cos the doctor said I weren't very well. I had

120

something called the mumps that makes you get really fat. (*VINCE blows out his cheeks.*) I asked my mum if my Uncle Richard had mumps all the time, 'cos he's always really, really fat. But she got annoyed and said he didn't have mumps, and that it's not his fault he's fat. The reason he's so big is that he suffers from his glands. I think he's fat 'cos he's always eating big bags of pickled onion monster munch, which make you really fat and really smelly. But I kept that to myself. Then my daddy said it was good for me to get mumps now anyway, 'cos if I got them when I was older it wouldn't just be my cheeks that would blow up into the size of tennis balls. I don't know what he meant. Adults always have to be so *mysterious*.

Anyway, I'm better now and back at school, worst luck. My bestest friend at school is called Aaron. It used to be Liam but he's only my fourth-bestest friend now, 'cos the other week he wee'd in my packed lunch box for a laugh, but it wasn't very funny. The teacher told my mummy that he suffered from anti-social behaviour, and we should make allowances. So we did. Me and Aaron secretly put bogeys in his marmite sand-wiches, and we watched him eat them all! Ugghh!

Aaron is the coolest kid in our class and he makes everyone laugh. In the playground he wiggles his thingamajig at the girls and makes them all scream. And he always says really rude words – like 'sex'! We don't know what it means, but it sounds really cool and makes all the girls go, 'Umm! I'm telling Miss.'

All the girls in our class are really weird. They're always being silly and giggling and saying, 'Vince, Aaron – do you wanna play kiss chase?' Ugghh! No way! I'd never kiss a girl. They're all horrible and smell. My dad says that one day I won't be able to get enough of kissing girls, not once my 'ormones kick in. I don't know what 'ormones are but I don't like the sound of them. They'll probably be even worse than catching mumps. I don't want 'ormones. I want to stay like this, but with no girls, or teachers or adults saying, 'Oo's a big boy!'

Just me and Aaron, on our own, seven and three-quarters for ever. Yeah, that would be the coolest.

(*We hear a recording of* BRITNEY'S *voice, made with gaps to allow* VINCE *to respond.*)

BRITNEY:	Vince!
VINCE:	Oh no, it's Britney Wallis!
BRITNEY:	– VINCE!!
VINCE:	What?
BRITNEY:	I know a secret.
VINCE:	What?
BRITNEY:	Amy Bridges fancies you.
VINCE:	So?
BRITNEY:	She wants to kiss you.
VINCE:	Ughh! No way – she's a girl! I ain't kissing a girl.
BRITNEY:	Ooohh!! That means you like kissing boys!
VINCE:	No I don't!
BRITNEY:	Yes you do!
VINCE:	Don't!
BRITNEY:	DO!
VINCE:	DON'T!
BRITNEY:	DO!

(*Together*)

VINCE:	Don't, don't, don't, don't.
BRITNEY:	Do, do, do, do.

BRITNEY:	So what shall I tell Amy, then?
VINCE:	You can tell her – she smells!
BRITNEY:	You're so immature!
VINCE:	(*Mimics*) 'You're so immature.' I tell you – women! You can't live with 'em . . .

(*Music plays to fade as* VINCE *shuffles out.*)

122

 **SEVEN STAGES OF MAN**

22. Part Three: The Stud Muffin

'I move around the dance floor, looking ultra cool,
Sending vibes out to all the ladies – tonight Vince
is on the pull.'

Props

Costume

Baggy jeans
Trainers
Hooded top

Sound

Club music
Recorded dialogue

(*Musical intro in dance/club style.* VINCE *enters as a 19-year-old trendy clubber, wearing baggy jeans, trainers and hooded top.* VICKY *and* SANDRA's *voices are recorded with gaps to allow* VINCE *to respond.*)

SANDRA: 'Ere, Vicky – see Vince Hunter over there?
VICKY: Oh yeah.
SANDRA: He's well fit, ain't he?
VICKY: He's all right, I suppose.
SANDRA: Good dancer as well.
VICKY: You're joking! It looks like he's got diarrhoea.
SANDRA: Oh don't be horrible, Vicks! I well fancy him.
VICKY: All right, keep your wig on. I'll ask him out for you . . .

VICKY: All right, Vince?
VINCE: All right, Vicks.
VICKY: You on your own?
VINCE: Not for much longer, darling.
VICKY: Oh yeah? Do you know my mate Sandra?
VINCE: Who?
VICKY: Sandra! Over there with the Bacardi Breezer.
VINCE: Oh yeah, the tart from the building society.
VICKY: She well fancies you.
VINCE: Well, who can blame her?
VICKY: Don't know why, myself.
VINCE: 'Cos I'm so sexy, Vicks. I can't help it.
VICKY: Huh! So, are you interested, then?
VINCE: Maybe later. I'm keeping my options open at the mo.

124

VICKY: Misogynist pig!
VINCE: Love you too, Vicky. Silly moo!

(*Dance music gets louder.* VINCE *dances, then the music suddenly stops.* VINCE *delivers the next lines as a rhyme with force and passion.*)

VINCE

I'm now a virile 19-year-old in the prime of misspent
    youth,
My mother thinks I'm common as muck and generally
    uncouth.

My bedroom is my castle, bedecked with cut-out Yodas;
It has a whiff of Paco Rabanne and rancid bodily odours.

I run my own top business, with my chamois doing
    windows;
I like to mount my ladder and wolf-whistle all the bimbos.

I frequent the local nightclubs, I go out on the prowl,
On the shufti for a slapper who applies her make-up with a
    trowel.

I move around the dance floor, looking ultra cool,
Sending vibes out to the ladies – tonight Vince is on the
    pull.

Right! She's too porky, she's too skinny, ooh that one looks
    like Mystic Meg!
She's all spotty, she's well grotty, that old moo's got hairy
    legs!

I settle for this bird Sandra, I'd give her a seven or eight;
In the morning, if she's minging, I'll go with Vicky, her
    best mate!

(*Blast of music, short and loud, stops suddenly.*)

Sandra! Sandra! Darling! Anytime you're ready!

(*To audience*) She's upstairs getting ready. Look – while I'm waiting, if there's any boys out there, get your notebooks out and learn from Vince, the Love Maestro.

Ready? Right – now, as an example, let's take Sandra, my new bird. Fell prey to my charms a few months back. Now, I chatted it up one lunchtime when I was doing the windows of the building society she works at, right? That same evening I treated her to an *à la carte* doner kebab. Invited her back to mine, stuck me 'Now That's What I Call Music' CD on and knocked her sideways!

(*Quick blast of music.*)

Anyway, the boys I hang out with (the Highbury mafia, they call us – a right bunch of desperadoes!) – they couldn't pull a bird if she had one arm and a winch!

(*Mimics mates*) 'Vince!' they say. 'How do you manage it with the birds, mate?'

'I dunno,' I say. 'I think the phrase you're looking for is "animal magnetism"!'

The only reason such a suave, sophisticated guy like me hangs out with this bunch of yobbish losers is for our Saturday afternoon soirées at Highbury Stadium. We all pile in the North Stand, sink a few pints, have a bit of a laugh – can't be bad.

I tell you, it's a bit of a change from childhood – going shopping with your mum and having to visit your granny. What a muppet! Some things stay the same, though. I still hang out with my best mate, Aaron – he hasn't changed, still the life and soul of the party. Still flashing his teeth at the girls – he hasn't got a clue, that boy. My success with the fairer sex comes from knowing how to treat 'em well – know what I mean? Here, watch – *Sandra!! What the 'ek are you doing up there?*

SANDRA

All right, all right! I'm going as fast as I can!

VINCE

Easy girl, easy!

Treat 'em mean, keep 'em keen – that's my motto. She's up there at the mo, tarting herself up with her best mate, Vicky! Vicky, who wears skirts the width of a bit of dental floss, applies her make-up with a trowel and just about managed to scrape one GCSE in needlework!

Can't complain, though. Sandra's a good girl. She said to me the other day (*impersonates Sandra*), 'Ooh Vince, do you know why I love you so much?' Well, I would have answered, but it could have been one of a thousand things, so I let her go on. (*Continues impression*) 'I love you 'cos you're such a modern man!'

Now, I wouldn't have thought of that, but, give it a bit of credit, she's quite right, 'cos I am in touch with my more caring and feminine side.

Example: last Friday I treated her out to a slap-up fish and chip supper. Now, I only got about halfway through mine, 'cos my guts were giving me gyp. My own fault – I'd had six pints and a dodgy curry the night before. Anyway, Miss Sarky Moo says, 'Ooh, what a waste! There's millions starving in Africa who'd give their right arm for that.' So, without thinking, and in hindsight rather stupidly, I chucked it at her and said, 'Well, send it to them, then.'

Now, as soon as I said it I realised how daft it sounded, 'cos it's not really practical to shove a half-eaten tray of haddock, chips and mushy peas into a jiffy bag and send it to Africa. For a start, who would you send it to? Genghis Khan? Muppetma Gandhi? Winston Mandela?

Anyway, I felt a bit guilty afterwards, 'cos she's a good girl, Sandra – thick as a plank, but nice, you know? My mum and dad love her! It's all 'Ooh hello, Sandra. How're you keeping, love?' 'Oh, fine, thank you, Mrs Hunter, Mr Hunter.' Makes you sick. Mum said to me the other day, 'I don't know how you managed to get such a lovely, intelligent girlfriend as Sandra.' Intelligent! She must be mad. I was, like, 'Yeah, thanks, Mum.' I mean, loyalty! I love my mum to bits – well, she's my mum, ain't she? – but I don't think she's ever quite realised what a total 100 per cent stud muffin she's managed to produce. I mean easy, girls – easy!

(*Blast of music as* VINCE *exits.*)

 **SEVEN STAGES OF MAN**

23. Part Four: The Wife and Kids

'I'm still clinging on to my youth. The thread is
tenuously thin, but it's still there.'

Props

Costume   *Sound*

Adidas top   'When I'm cleaning windows'
Silver ring
Towel

(*Musical introduction relating to the working man, eg 'When I'm cleaning windows'.* VINCE *enters as a young dad, wearing Adidas top, carrying a towel and kids' paraphernalia. He is wiping sick from his top.*)

VINCE

Ah, Sand! He's done it again, ain't he! Every flaming time! Oh, don't give me all that 'he's just a baby' rubbish – he knows!

If I have the rag conveniently placed on my shoulder, does he ever puke? No. But if I'm wearing my favourite Adidas top, fresh out the wash, you can guarantee he's gonna barf all over it. I mean look – that stain ain't gonna come out, not in a million years.

*   *   *

You know, when I was a kiddy, adults used to do my nut in saying stuff like, 'Ooh, where do the years go?' and 'Time just flies by.' I used to wanna grab hold of them and their banal philosophies and say, 'Oh, shut up, you pranny!' But the funny old thing is, they were right. Ironic, innit?

But I'm still clinging on to my youth. The thread is tenuously thin, but it's still there. I'm as fit as a fiddle, no worries on that front. (*Starts shadow-boxing, which ends with an obvious twinge.*) Yeah, mid-thirties and proud of it. I'm not sure when it officially becomes late thirties, but I'll stick with mids if it's all the same to you, right?

* * *

Have you noticed the new silverware? (*Indicates wedding ring.*) Sandra and I got hitched – oh, seven years ago. Or maybe it was eight, or nine; anyway, something like that.

I must admit the whole thing wasn't overly romantic. It was Sandra's idea. She insisted I made an honourable woman out of her . . . which was a bit ripe, being that she was six months up the duff at the time with our first boy, Jason.

Our new little spawn, the projectile vomiter, is our third – Arthur. And in the middle we had little Holly. But that's the lot now. Three is plenty. Anyone who has more is just a glutton for punishment, in my opinion.

Anyway, plans are afoot on my part, you know. Snippity-snip, if you catch my drift. Don't get me wrong, though: I love my kids to bits. Anyone messes with them and that'll be it for 'em. And, give them credit, most of the time they're really good. It's just sometimes they do my head in. I don't feel like killing them on a regular basis – maybe only once a week, twice tops.

It's the whining that does me in – 'Dad, Jason did this', 'But she did it first', 'Can we do this?', 'Can we go there?', 'I want such-and-such!' There's only so much I can take. What I don't understand is, they can see me watching the Arsenal on the telly, right, so is it likely that I'll want to make a play-dough model or help Holly create a girly friendship bangle? No – I've always got my standard answer ready, and it's a good one. Whatever the request, the answer is, 'Go and ask your mum.' Don't matter what they say, it's the same. 'Go and ask your mum.' Works a treat, I tell you. Sandra loves it!

* * *

I don't know what I'd do without her, Sandra. She's a rock – a rock! Moany old bag quite a lot of the time, but nevertheless

131

a rock. When you get together with someone, if you get it right, you never quite realise what a goldmine you've struck. I didn't, anyway. Not that I'd tell her that. When I'm with Sandra it just seems so . . . natural. I can totally be myself. I don't know why, but I just can. When we're together, alone, we sit and talk for hours, we laugh, no subject is taboo. Just being together is so . . . And then the kids come in and it's all 'Entertain me, amuse me, give me all your attention!' And of course we do.

I do this trick for them, with a glass of water, a biscuit-tin lid, a matchbox and an egg – don't ask! My dad used to do it for me, and his for him all the way back.

* * *

He died last year, my dad. Only 62. Nothing, is it? Not in this day and age anyway. Colorectal cancer. He never let on, not even to my mum. 'What's the point in upsetting everyone? There's nothing you can do.' Daft old duffer! Makes you stop and think, though. One minute he's there, seemingly indestructible – my dad! Then I find myself standing at his grave, carrying a suitcase of regrets and missed opportunities. 'Ooh, where do the years go?' Makes you think, don't it?

(*Music plays as* VINCE *exits.*)

 **SEVEN STAGES OF MAN**

24. Part Five: Flying the Nest

'Kids, eh! Who'd have 'em? How can something
that is meant to bring you such joy cause
such pain?'

Props

Costume	Sound
Suit and tie	Heavy rock music
Briefcase	'As time goes by'
	'Sound of silence'
	Recorded dialogue

(*Musical introduction on the theme of passing years, eg 'As time goes by'. VINCE enters as a businessman wearing a jacket and tie, carrying a case. Voices of SANDRA, HOLLY and ARTHUR are pre-recorded, with gaps for VINCE.*)

SANDRA: Darling, the central heating's packed in. Can you take a look?

VINCE: Yeah, okay, will do.

ARTHUR: Dad, I need a lift into town tonight. Can you take us?

VINCE: Ask your mother, will you?

HOLLY: Dad, the oil light's come up on my car. Can you sort it?

VINCE: Yeah, I'll show you what to do later.

ARTHUR: Dad, Mum says to ask you to take me into town.

VINCE: Oh well, we'll see.

SANDRA: Did you bring home that milk, love?

VINCE: Oh, sorry, I forgot.

HOLLY: Ooh, Dad, someone called for you earlier; said it was urgent.

VINCE: Who was it?

HOLLY: Can't remember.

VINCE: Oh, Holly!

SANDRA: Love, can you take Arthur into town later? I've got my yoga class.

VINCE: I suppose so.

SANDRA: And get the milk on your way back.

134

VINCE:	Yes, dear! Anything, dear!
ALL:	Dad! Dad! Darling! Dad!
VINCE:	*Aaagghh! Shut up!*

(*Sudden silence.*)

VINCE

Can you hear that? The sound of silence . . . (*A quick blast of Simon and Garfunkel, drowned out by heavy rock*) *Arthur! Will you turn that racket down?!*

I'm a martyr to them all, do you know that? An absolute martyr. You've heard of a 'lull before the storm' – well, this is the final storm before the lull, and believe me it's a typhoon. Give it just a few more years and they'll all be gone, standing on their own two feet – or not, as the case may be.

The business is going well. Branched out from the windows about ten years back. Doing carpet-cleaning now, curtains, a few office contracts – very nice. Even got a few employees now, which is a stroke of luck, given the state of my knees. Every time I bend down I sound like a pair of castanets! (*Demonstrates this*) Sandra does the tax, which is a bit of a laugh, seeing as she flunked her maths GCSE twice! Still, no fines yet, so I can't complain.

Come September, Holly's off to university – imagine that, little Holly, university. First one in our family ever. You gotta be proud. I just wish Mum and Dad had lived to see it . . . his face would have been a picture! She's going up to the university in Liverpool. I said to her, 'Liverpool! What do you wanna go all the way up there for? You'll be miles away from us!' She just looked at me and smiled knowingly. Liverpool! I ask you. It's a different language up there, innit!

The course she's doing is some postmodern studies thing. Can't remember exactly. Sounds like a bit of a skive. Probably is a bit of a skive – I mean what sort of job can you get with that? She says it's perfect; perfect for a full-time career as a lifestyle guru. Lifestyle guru – it beggars belief!

Still, at least she's driven. I'll give her credit for that – she's very driven.

And Arthur – remember baby Arthur, the projectile vomiter? – he's now a full-on moody teenager. I don't tend to have a great deal of conversation with him. He normally communicates using a series of grunts, burps and farts. Still, all par for the course, I suppose. He thinks he hates us, certainly acts like he hates us – but he doesn't. No, my theory is when a teenager's going through their rebellious 'I hate my parents' phase, that's really when deep down they need you most. Freudian, eh! Of course, Arthur doesn't realise that, nor any other teenager – no, if they did, it would upset the yin and yang of the whole concept. So suffer we do!

He's in with another three or four knuckleheads at his school. Set up some heavy metal grunge band. Call themselves 'Puss'! Need I say more? They had their first gig last week, hired the community centre, played to 16 people, including the caretaker. I was meaning to go, but I had a sudden unquenchable desire to pluck my eyebrows, so I had to give it a miss. Sandra went, to show a bit of maternal support. Came back about an hour later, shaking, ears bleeding – she's not been the same since, poor thing. Still, serves her right for trying to be all trendy and relevant!

And then there's our Jason . . . dear Jason . . . the firstborn. The lost son. We don't know where he is. No idea! Packed his bags long ago, nearly three years now. Made his pitch to conquer the world. Didn't quite work like that, though, did it? Not with what he got caught up in – the crowd, the drugs, the vice . . . I often wonder if I'd even recognise him, after three years on the street. Sandra says she would. Reckons she could spot him in a crowd any time, any place. She probably could, too. Don't know if I could, though. I think about him every day. Of course I do, all the time; but his face is still fast fading. You eventually get used to not seeing it.

There is communication. He phones, which is something, I suppose. Better than most in our position. Yeah, once every

136

few months he calls. Always the same – he's off his face on I don't know what. Shouting down the phone to us, 'Give us some money, give me money, *I need money*!' And I try to tell him no, we don't want him spending money on any of that stuff – them drugs. So he yells again and again, 'I hate you, I hate you, *I hate you*!'

Now, I'm pretty tough, but we all have our limits – you know what I mean? So of course I back down. It doesn't take long. Offer to send him what he needs, get the details of where to transfer it this time – London, Manchester, Brighton. And then we get back our little Jason, just for a few seconds. 'Thanks,' he says. 'I love you, Mum. I love you, Dad.' And then he's gone. It's killing Sandra. Slowly, it's killing her . . .

*   *   *

I don't know. Kids, eh! Who'd have 'em? How can something that is meant to bring you such joy cause such pain? What's happening, God? If you're there, sort it out!

Bit of a cheek, I know, only asking when things are tough. I just never thought about you much before. Never needed to.

There's gotta be some rhyme and reason to all of this, hasn't there? Hasn't there?

(*Music plays.* VINCE *freezes for a few seconds then exits.*)

137

 **SEVEN STAGES OF MAN**

25. Part Six: OAP Blues

'My whole body is groaning, with some extremely
worrying noises.'

Props

Costume	*Sound*
Cardigan	Blues track
Slippers	

(*Musical introduction, playing the blues.* VINCE *enters as an OAP, wearing slippers and a cardigan. He is limping, and suddenly his knee gives out.*)

VINCE

Oh no, not again! Sandra! The flaming thing's seized up again! Sandra! Oh, for the love of . . . grapes! Well, I'm due a rest anyway. (*VINCE carefully sits down.*)

You've heard of tennis elbow – well, this is window cleaner's knee. Yeah, all that upping and downing ladders, freeing you lot from grime, giving you a sparkly clean outlook on life, takes its toll, and don't forget it!

I mean, what's the point of having a knee if it can't complete its most basic function? It's only got to go like that, for crying out loud. (*Demonstrates knee movement using his hand*) It's not rocket science, is it? But no! Mine's on strike. It's like, 'No, I refuse to flex. I will remain rigid until I am given recognition as a major organ of the body.'

It's not just my knee that's on strike either, no – I wish! My whole body is groaning, with some extremely worrying noises. And I'm not being rude, but I'm making more than my fair share of those noises too! I'm slowing up, fading out, winding down. Everything needs a good service, but it's got to that stage where you think, what's the flipping point? I'm on a permanent go-slow. I wanna speed up but I can't. The only faculty that does speed up is your bladder. Ironic really. The one thing you want to slow down is the only thing that speeds up! I'm a four-visits-a-night man, at least, without fail. Can't remember my last uninterrupted night – what I'd give for a good night's sleep . . .

140

OAP. I'm an OAP! I'm an old, aged pensioner. Charming description, isn't it? Very flattering. It's not enough to call us just 'old' or 'elderly', they have to ram the point home – you're an old, aged, ancient pensioner. As if I need reminding of the fact, what with my knees! Oh, and I was in Tesco the other day, looking at their wide range of tinned meats, and I turned round to look at their special offer display, two-for-one on Fray Bentos corned beef, and my neck just froze. I was like that for half an hour. Sandra had to guide me over to the little café thing and finish the week's shop on her own. I ask you . . .

* * *

We're on our own now, just the two of us – you've probably gathered. All flown the nest, years ago now. Holly's over in America, doing very well advising people on feng shoe, and how to make the most of your life! Even written a book now, would you believe? Sold a few copies, I think. She never comes home. New beginnings, I suppose. But she calls. Yeah, she calls once every few . . . well, not very often, I suppose.

Arthur's doing well, got himself hitched, lives in Carlisle. Never been quite sure why, but there you go. And our Jason – well, who knows. Who knows where he is. I'm still looking for some answers, lots of answers. Can't find them. Sandra thinks that deep down I don't want to find them, too scared in case I don't like what I find. Maybe she's right, but I'm sure she's not. I *do* want to know. What's it all for? I'm beginning to understand why those people sing the blues . . .

(*A blues riff cuts in. VINCE sings the blues in a style of something like Elvis Presley's 'Trouble'.*)

If you're looking for trouble, boy you're in the right place,
If you're looking for trouble, just look in my face,
I was born in an egg box, just outside Milton Keynes,

141

Spent a lifetime on the windows and its knackered out my
    knees.

Oh, I am ancient, my middle name is misery.
Oh, I'm an OAP, so don't you mess around with me.

When you get to my age, things start to click,
Mostly my neck, ah, it makes you sick.
My prostate is hopeless, the whole thing's a farce,
I suffer with chronic piles, it's a right pain in the . . . neck.

Oh, I am ancient, my middle name is misery.
Oh, I'm an OAP, so don't you mess around with me.

(*For final verse and chorus the blues still plays but in a more
melancholic style, changing feel from comic to tragic.*)

Was an orphan by 50, my family's a mess.
Eldest son done a runner, left no forwarding address.
The other two scarpered, spread out their wings,
We love 'em all to pieces, but the phone, it rarely rings.

Oh, I am ancient, my middle name is misery.
Oh, I'm an OAP, so don't you mess around with me.

(*VINCE exits as music continues to a fade.*)

 **SEVEN STAGES OF MAN**

26. Part Seven: Mere Oblivion

'The circle of life. From the first stages of
helplessness to the final stages of helplessness,
and everything in between.'

Props

Costume

Pyjamas
Dressing gown
Slippers

Sound

Mournful music
Recorded dialogue

(*Music of an emotive, mournful style. VINCE enters, shuffling on in pyjamas and dressing gown. He sits slumped centre stage. The voice of the NURSE is pre-recorded.*)

NURSE

Are you all right, Mr Hunter?

Mr Hunter?

Had enough, have we?

Have you finished, Mr Hunter? (*VINCE groans.*)

Yeah, you have a rest now, then.

Have a nice little nap and I'll come to see you later. (*VINCE groans.*)

Behave yourself now! Don't do anything I wouldn't do ... you hear?

VINCE

In the words of Shakespeare – 'cos I'm a bit of a culture vulture, me – I was brought into this world mewling and puking in the nurse's arms. And by the looks of it, I'm gonna be going out the self-same way. I suppose there's some kind of ironic poetry in that. The circle of life. From the first stages of helplessness to the final stages of helplessness, and everything in between.

Once again, all dignity is stripped. I'm laid bare, quite literally. It's hard to retain much sense of pride when you're being helped to the toilet by a 17-year-old with no qualifications – no, that's unfair. They're very good here, very caring. Always have a joke with you, especially when

144

you're in a rather compromising position. Frumpy Frieda's the best one. Her favourite little catchphrase is, 'Don't do anything I wouldn't do!' Of course it loses its punch after the first 50 times, but at least she makes the effort.

And all the carers do like a bit of fun and games. And I don't blame them – the misery they have to witness daily, and on their hourly rate, they need something to cheer them up! They do this one game with us catatonics, where they prop us up on our seat then take bets on which way we'll slump first – to the left or to the right. Keeps them amused for hours, that one. And I suppose I can see why, in a funny sort of way.

* * *

George went last week. Had the bedroom opposite me; used to always sit by the window over there. He had a rather strange propensity to burst into sudden renditions of Pavarotti arias. Most entertaining! The place has been a lot quieter without him, but ever so slightly dull!

There's not much to do in here, except think. Eat, sleep and think. Four years now – four and counting. Four years since Sandra and I had to admit defeat; we couldn't cope any more. There was no question of living with either of the kids, both so busy, Holly still abroad even. Arthur has his own family now, three kids. He was very apologetic, of course, but we told him not to be so daft: 'You've got your own life to lead,' we said. And if the truth be known, I really didn't fancy moving to Carlisle. Much too far west for my liking. No, so we both signed up for the knacker's yard – well, everything done for you, meals, cleaning and a nice little double room overlooking the gardens . . . or so we thought. So we were led to believe.

Of course they apologised most sincerely. These instances were extremely rare, but it was a sign of the times. Social service budget cuts, lack of NHS resources, all the classic excuses. But it amounted to the same thing – they had to separate us. Didn't have a place that could accommodate both of us. Ridiculous really, but I didn't have the strength to argue, not any more.

'Of course we'll see what we can do, arrange visits in the meantime.' But that was hardly the point. I remember the morning they picked us up, carted us off! Most of our belongings had gone ahead; we just clutched one little bag each. We sat in the back of this car, holding hands in silence. Didn't say anything, not a word. Couldn't think what to say. When we got to Sandra's . . . new home, these nurses started to help her out of the car and she resisted. She was struggling and they virtually had to drag her out, and she was screaming, 'Don't leave me, Vince! Stay with me! I need you to stay with me!'

And I didn't do a thing; just looked at her. They were saying, 'Don't worry, Mrs Hunter. Come with us now and you'll see Mr Hunter a bit later.' But she still struggled. She was having none of it. 'Don't leave me, Vince, please!'

The car pulled away, and I saw her through the rear window, slowly fading to nought.

* * *

She died two weeks later. Thirteen days, to be precise. Funny really, she was always the more healthy. They think she died of . . . a broken heart. I was hot favourite to follow her within the month; apparently that's what usually happens to us helpless husbands. But I've defied the odds. I'm hanging in there, in my cocoon.

The kids visit when they can, but it's a right old trek for them. I hope I'm not too much of an inconvenience. No, mostly it's just me and Frumpy Frieda nowadays . . . and my thoughts. Thoughts of a lost wife and son, of distant relatives, of a life lived. I question the point of it all, constantly; bit late now, I suppose.

Is there any meaning to it? Any rhyme and reason? And if God's up there, where's he been? What's next for us all . . . for me?

All the time these thoughts – oh, what's the point? *What's the point?*

(*Option:* recite the 'seven ages of man' speech from Shakespeare's *As You Like It.*)

(*Mournful music plays as* VINCE *returns to catatonic state. Lights fade to blackout.*)

PART
4

BIBLE CHARACTERS

27. The Biggest Laugh

'Well, I couldn't control myself, could I! You
know that feeling when you know you really
shouldn't laugh, but you can't help yourself!'

SARAH

I've always wanted kids. In my experience most women do. I know that many can live happy and fulfilled lives without, but I just wasn't one of them. And I know what a lot of hassle they can be – new-born babies, throwing up all over the place, screaming the house down, marmalade dripping all down your walls! And it doesn't stop there: all the way through to the moody teenage years and beyond it's one trial after another. But they were trials I was prepared to undertake, to welcome even. But the best-laid plans, so they say . . .

We tried, for years we tried, my husband Abe and I, but nothing. No, everyone around me seemed to be falling pregnant at the drop of a hat – all my friends, my neighbours, my brothers' wives – seemingly everyone except me. And it hurt. Somehow I felt incomplete, a failure. Abe tried to cheer me up, saying, 'It's just not meant to be,' and that maybe it was his fault, not mine, but I knew it wasn't. I knew it was me. I was barren, and I felt so guilty. Abe would so obviously be a wonderful father, but I, his wife, could not provide him with children.

To be fair, everyone around us was terrific. Family and friends all so supportive, no sly or snide comments, not to my face anyway, but just so many pitying looks. Poor Sarah. Poor childless Sarah. And that pity, well-meant as it was, cut me to the bone.

* * *

But, as with so many things, time to a certain extent proved to be the healer. As I moved into my autumn years, the thought of motherhood became nothing more than a wistful distant dream. I could hardly complain, anyway: God had richly blessed me in so many other areas of my life. I was satisfied now to enter a relaxing retirement – or so I thought.

It was just at this time that Abe and I received three visitors. And, as it turned out, they were messengers from God.

Abe kept them talking while I prepared them a meal of pancakes, roast veal, cheese and milk to drink. Just as I was about to take it in to them I heard them talking from the other side of the door. And one of them said, 'Next year I will give you and Sarah a son.' Well, I couldn't control myself, could I! You know that feeling when you know you really shouldn't laugh, but you just can't help yourself! Well, I felt the laughter rise up, and it was impossible to stifle it. When confronted about it I said I didn't laugh, but of course I did.

I mean, imagine it! A woman my age having a baby! And with a husband as old as mine is! Come on, get real – we're both in our eighties – *early* eighties I grant you, but still just a tad past childbearing years.

But the messenger was insistent. 'Is anything too hard for God? Next year, just as I have said, Sarah will have a son.'

* * *

I should have believed it straight away, no questions asked. I know that now. Normally I'm a woman of great faith, but somehow I struggled to take this at face value – understandably, maybe. The promise of a son, the descendants that would be numbered like stars – it seemed so impossible. So I tried to make it possible, give God a helping hand you might say. I gave over my young maidservant, Hagar, to sleep with my husband. She could get pregnant, we could bring the child up as our own, and then Abe could have what he was due. If you're listening to this in another place and another time, you might think that sounds a bit strange, downright immoral even – but I can assure you, where I come from it's common practice. Nobody even bats an eyelid. And it worked. My plan succeeded: Hagar became pregnant and for a time it all seemed so perfect.

But it was then that I started to feel uncomfortable. A discomfort I'd dreamt about for so many years. A swelling, a certain sickness – those first pangs of pregnancy . . .

151

* * *

Why did I ever doubt?

How could I lack faith? I, who believe so much in my God who created everything, who has a plan for me that is good and perfect. Yet at the crucial moment I failed to believe that a miracle could be performed in me, within me.

And later, when the child was born, we named him Isaac, meaning laughter. And I told everyone, 'God has brought me "laughter".' Because who could have dreamed that Abe and I would have a baby in our old age? And our child brings us such joy, despite the difficulties brought on by my hurried efforts at problem-solving.

How foolish I was not to believe completely in the promise of God.

How foolish to try to help him along with his plans.

Maybe, after all this is sorted out, the biggest laugh will be on me.

Bible reference: Genesis 17

⚡ BIBLE CHARACTERS

28. Jesus (Part One)
From Matthew's Gospel Account

Introduction

Given the challenge of writing a monologue of Jesus, I must admit I rather balked! It didn't rest easy to write words into Jesus's mouth in the same style I do for other characters. The result was the next two pieces. Using a red-letter NKJV Bible I sourced all of Jesus's words, and then tried to create something meaningful. I hope you like the outcome. When I've read these out, the response has been positive. It certainly shows just how powerful Christ's words were and are.

16:13	Who do people say that the Son of Man is?
16:15	Who do you say that I am?

* * *

7:7	Ask and it shall be given to you; seek, and you will find; knock and it will be opened to you.
4:4	Man shall not live by bread alone, but by every word that comes from the mouth of God.
4:17	Repent, for the Kingdom of Heaven is at hand.
4:19	Follow me, and I will make you fishers of men.
5:14	You are the light of the world.
7:1	Judge not, that you be not judged.
5:43–44	You have heard that it was said, you shall love your neighbour and hate your enemy. But I say to you, love your enemies and pray for those who persecute you.
5:46–47	For if you love those who love you, what reward do you have? Do not even the tax collectors do the same? And if you only greet your brothers, what more are you doing than others? Do not even the gentiles do the same?
22:37–39	You shall love the Lord your God with all your heart and with all your soul and with all your mind. This is the first and greatest command-

154

ment. And a second is like it: love your neighbour as yourself.

6:19–21   Do not lay up for yourselves treasures on earth, where moth and rust destroy and where thieves break in and steal, but lay up for yourselves treasure in heaven, where neither moth nor rust destroys and where thieves do not break in and steal. For where your treasure is, there your heart will be also.

6:25   Do not be anxious about your life, what you will eat or what you will drink, nor about your body, what you will put on.

6:34   Do not be anxious about tomorrow, for tomorrow will be anxious for itself. Sufficient for the day is its own trouble.

6:5   And when you pray, you must not be like the hypocrites, for they love to stand and pray in the synagogues and at the street corners, that they may be seen by others. Truly, I say to you, they have received their reward.

23:13   Woe to you, scribes and Pharisees, hypocrites! For you shut the Kingdom of Heaven in people's faces. For you neither enter yourselves nor allow those who would enter to go in.

23:27   Woe to you, scribes and Pharisees, hypocrites! For you are like whitewashed tombs, which outwardly appear beautiful but within are full of dead people's bones and all uncleanness.

18:7   Woe to the world for temptations to sin! For it is necessary that temptations come, but woe to the one by whom the temptation comes.

10:34   Do not think that I have come to bring peace to the earth. I have not come to bring peace, but a sword.

5:17–18   Do not think that I have come to abolish the law or the prophets; I have not come to abolish

155

them but to fulfil them. For truly I say to you, until heaven and earth pass away, not an iota, not a dot, will pass from the law until all is accomplished.

7:21–23 Not everyone who says to me 'Lord, Lord' will enter the Kingdom of Heaven. On that day many will say to me, 'Lord, Lord, did we not prophesy in your name, and cast out demons in your name, and do many mighty works in your name?' And then I will declare to them, 'I never knew you.'

10:26–27 So have no fear of them, for nothing is covered that will not be revealed, or hidden that will not be known. What I tell you in the dark, say in the light, and what you hear whispered, proclaim on the housetops.

10:32–33 So everyone who acknowledges me before men, I also will acknowledge before my Father who is in Heaven, but whoever denies me before men, I also will deny before my Father who is in Heaven.

10:16–18 I am sending you out as sheep in the midst of wolves, so be wise as serpents and innocent as doves. Beware of men, for they will deliver you over to courts and flog you in their synagogues, and you will be dragged before governors and kings for my sake, to bear witness before them and the gentiles.

11:28–30 Come to me, all who labour and are heavy laden, and I will give you rest. Take my yoke upon you, and learn from me, for I am gentle and lowly in heart, and you will find rest for your souls. For my yoke is easy and my burden is light.

19:26 With men this is impossible, but with God all things are possible.

☼ BIBLE CHARACTERS

29. Jesus (Part Two)
From Matthew's Gospel Account

16:15	Who do you say that I am?
16:13	Who do people say that the Son of Man is?

*   *   *

17:22–23	The Son of Man is about to be delivered into the hands of man, and they will kill him.
20:18–19	The Son of Man will be delivered over to the chief priests and scribes, and they will condemn him to death and deliver him over to the gentiles to be mocked and flogged and crucified and he will be raised on the third day.
26:18	My time is at hand. I will keep the Passover . . . with my disciples.
26:21	Truly I say to you, one of you will betray me.
26:23	He who has dipped his hand in the dish with me will betray me.
26:31	You will all fall away because of me this night.
26:34	I tell you, this very night, before the cock crows, you will deny me three times.
26:26	Take, eat: this is my body.
26:27	Drink of it, all of you, for this is my blood of the covenant which is poured out for many for the forgiveness of sins. I tell you I will not drink again of this fruit of the vine until that day when I drink it with you in my Father's Kingdom.
26:38	My soul is very sorrowful, even to death; remain here and watch with me.
26:39	My Father, if it be possible, let this cup pass from me; nevertheless not as I will, but as you will.
26:42	My Father, if this cannot pass unless I drink it, your will be done.
26:23	He who has dipped his hand in the dish with me will betray me.

| 26:50 | Friend, do what you came to do. |
| 26:52 | Put your sword back into its place. For all who take the sword will perish by the sword. |

* * *

| 16:13 | Who do people say that the Son of Man is? |
| 16:15 | Who do you say that I am? |

* * *

26:64	You have said so. But I tell you, from now on, you will see The Son of Man seated at the right hand of Power and coming on the clouds of heaven.
24:29–31	The sun will be darkened and the moon will not give its light and the stars will fall from heaven, and the powers of the heavens will be shaken. Then will appear in heaven the signs of the Son of Man, and then all the tribes of the earth will mourn, and they will see the Son of Man coming on the clouds of heaven with power and great glory. And he will send all his angels with a loud trumpet call, and they will gather his elect from the four winds, from one end of heaven to another.
24:36	But concerning that day and hour no one knows, not even the angels of heaven, nor the Son, but the Father only.
17:22	The Son of Man is about to be delivered into the hands of man, and they will kill him.
27:46	Eloi, eloi, lama sabachthani? My God, my God, why have you forsaken me?
14:27	Take heart. It is I.
14:31	O you of little faith, why did you doubt?
17:22	The Son of Man is about to be delivered into

the hands of men, and they will kill him, and he will be raised on the third day.

27:63   After three days I will rise again.

* * *

16:13   Who do people say that the Son of Man is?
16:15   Who do you say that I am?

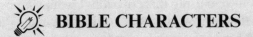 **BIBLE CHARACTERS**

30. Honeyed Lips, Poisoned Heart

'The story begins, as so many do, with a man
falling deeply in love with a girl.'

DELILAH

They say that the most important thing we can do for others is to help bring out the best in them – to identify the areas in which they can excel, and then encourage them to nurture these things and push the boundaries. Sounds pretty fair. But, if you were using this criterion, I would suppose, in all fairness, that you would have to describe me as an abject failure. For me the flip side is more accurate: my life will be remembered for identifying an area of great strength but then doing all in my power to prevent it from flourishing. Still, give me some credit – at least I am incredibly persistent.

* * *

The story begins, as so many do, with a man falling deeply in love with a girl. In this case the man was called Samson and the girl – me – Delilah. We lived in the valley of Sorek, between the Mediterranean and Dead Seas. He was an Israelite and I a lowly Philistine, and as such the relationship was frowned upon. Samson always had an eye for us Philistine women; his lust, of course, was his downfall. And though many will say I was purely a temptress, it is not entirely true. I had very strong feelings for this incredibly mighty but surprisingly gentle man. Even with the family pressures and the conflict of culture I believe that, had things been very different, we could have worked. We could have worked.

* * *

OK, so I can't pull the wool over your eyes – I'm not squeaky clean. I admit that what happened was all my fault. I was greedy; it was as simple as that. Samson, with his brute strength, was a thorn in the side of the Philistine nation. The powers that be wanted him suppressed and in me they saw a way to do it. They knew his weakness was his infatuation with me, and they knew my weakness was . . . money. Well, to be precise, lots of money. So all the leaders of the nation offered me money – bags of silver shekels, untold riches! All I had to do was find the secret of his monumental strength. An easy task, you would think.

I knew from the outset, with a supreme and unshakeable confidence, that I could get the information they needed. But, to be honest, Samson did prove a harder nut to crack than I could ever have expected. Instead of finding out what I needed to know, I found myself in what could best be described as a kind of groundhog day!

It would start with my pleading with Samson to tell me why he was so strong and how he could be defeated. 'Oh, darling, come now. You wouldn't want to keep any secrets from your little diddums.' A little flutter of the eyelashes would follow and then he would proceed to spin some far-fetched yarn about having to be tied up with leather thongs or brand new ropes, which, once he was asleep, I would carry out. The army would then charge in to capture him, and he would break free, making me look a complete 'nana.

Time and again this happened – the pleading, the lies and the escape followed by my persistent complaining. 'How can you say you love me when you won't confide in me!' Emotional blackmail always wins through, and eventually my nagging wore him down. On my fourth attempt to gain the secret he finally told me the truth. His strength was in his hair and, if it was cut, he would be as weak as anyone else. So simple!

People think Samson must have been rather stupid to fall for my tricks. Maybe once, they say, but four times? Is it possible he had no idea what was happening? Who knows? But he wanted to believe. He was blinded by lust, maybe love. I've heard people call me 'the woman with honey on her lips and poison in her heart'. I like that – very poetic, don't you think?

Poor, foolish Samson, you might think, but it's so easy to be deceived by flattering and temptation. One way or another we all are.

*   *   *

As he slept that night with his head on my lap I arranged for
his head to be shaved. And as the army came to capture him
one last time, I called out, 'Samson, the Philistines are upon
you!' But this time he had no strength – he strained to break
free, but couldn't understand what had happened, and for
the first time I saw real fear in his eyes. They bound him tight
with bronze shackles and then gouged out his eyes. Then
they dragged him all the way to Gaza, some 20 miles south,
and put him to hard labour in the prison. Blind and defeated
– a sorry sight indeed.

*   *   *

And do I regret it? If I'd known then all I know now, would
I have done things differently? I don't know. Truly, I don't
know. Part of me is sorry, of course, but I am aware of my
fatal flaw.

Maybe one day I'll find out. Maybe I'll get a second
chance and meet someone whom I can help to be the best
they can be, whatever the cost, no strings attached.

But for poor Samson there is no second chance. Chained
and imprisoned, he has paid the ultimate price for his association with me. For his poor judgement. Unless, of course,
his hair grows back. In which case, who knows . . .

Bible reference: Judges 16

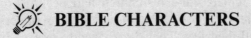 **BIBLE CHARACTERS**

31. The First Martyr

'And as the hate-filled stones thundered into
Stephen's head and body, crushing him,
he prayed . . .'

PHILIP

I first got to know him properly some time ago, when we were both selected to be part of a team administering a feeding programme to the poor in our area.

Since Jesus had ascended into heaven, his gospel had been widely circulated and his church had begun to grow at a great rate of knots! The disciples were understandably rushed off their feet. They'd managed to replace Judas with Matthias to take them back up to their original quota of twelve, but even so they needed to start delegating some of the more administrative roles. And that's where I came in – and Stephen, of course.

* * *

I can't describe to you my total shock and surprise when I was chosen to be one of the seven to supervise the food distribution. Especially when I heard that I would work alongside Stephen, whom everyone regarded highly for his qualities of faith, wisdom, grace and power. The others in our crack squad were Nicanor, Timon, Parmenas and Nicholaus of Antioch.

Now, before I continue, it might be worth mentioning this. You might imagine that a church so young, fresh and dynamic would be in a state of near-perfect grace, but I'm afraid I'll have to disappoint you. Even in those first, heady days we had our fair share of problems. With the number of believers growing rapidly every day, there was much in the way of mumbling and grumbling about who was getting preferential treatment in the distribution of food – and so this is the task we were charged with organising. And I believe, without being immodest, we did a pretty good job.

As I took my part in this task, I felt that my life was being shaped in a very definite way. For all of us, in our lives, from time to time, maybe only once, we meet someone so inspiring, so outstanding, we know we'll never be quite the same

166

again. For me, this person was Stephen. In everything he did, he strove for excellence, never attempting to cut corners but always completing things to the best of his ability. As a leader and a teacher and a debator he was unequalled in my circle and never failed to display the awesome power of the Holy Spirit in his life. He had a real understanding of God, and the practical nous and compassion to relate it to the people, and for that he was well loved. Ironically, this, of course, probably paved the way to his destruction.

*　*　*

Some men started an argument with him. They were from a Jewish cult and came from as far afield as Cyrene, Egypt, Cilicia and Asia Minor. As ever, it was an inspiration to see Stephen in action. Full of faith and with the Holy Spirit's power he debated them all into the ground. None could hold a candle to Stephen's wisdom. So, in a jealous rage, they concocted all manner of lies about him – accusations of his speaking against the Temple and cursing the name of Moses. They stoked up the crowds into a blazing fury, and succeeded in having him arrested. He was brought to Caiaphas – that same High Priest who not long before had questioned and condemned Christ himself.

As Stephen spoke to all the gathered council, his face shone like that of an angel. And he spoke with more wisdom and passion than ever before. He reminded them of the long history of Israel and of God's acts in the world. He told them that man had worshipped God long before the building of any temple, and that God does not live in a temple but in all the heavens and the earth. And he accused them of yet again rejecting God when they rejected his Son and killed him cruelly. And in all his many words that proved so offensive to their deaf ears he never spoke a single word in his own defence. Not because he forgot – but because he had no desire to. There was no need.

I suppose it was predictable that they would not – could not – tolerate his words. They ground their teeth in rage, planning unholy revenge. And as their tempers rose to boiling-point, Stephen just gazed to heaven. 'Look, I see the heavens opened and Jesus the Messiah standing beside God, at his right hand!'

These words were too much for them, so they mobbed him, an unruly gang drowning out his words with their shouts, and then they dragged him outside the city walls. Pushing him violently into a corner, they removed their coats and handed them to a zealot standing there named Saul. This Saul never struck Stephen or even said a word, but he looked on with great content as the others began to stone him. And as the hate-filled stones thundered into Stephen's head and body, crushing him, he prayed. 'Lord Jesus, receive my spirit. Lord Jesus, don't charge them with this sin.' Then he died. Our first martyr.

* * *

But he will not die in vain, this I vow. In fear of the inevitable repercussions I fled north to Samaria and I preached. Every opportunity I got, I preached. Then, last night, an angel spoke to me, sending me to this very road, the one that runs from Jerusalem through the Gaza desert. I have an appointment at noon, just five minutes from now . . . Who knows what's in store? Exciting, eh? In the far distance I think I can see some rising dust – maybe it's a chariot . . .

Bible reference: Acts 6–8

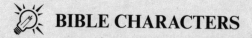 **BIBLE CHARACTERS**

32. Not So Rosy in the Garden

'Normally I'm a pretty sharp cookie, but he must
have caught me on a bit of an off-day.'

EVE

It all started off so very well. Perfection, you might even say! Always extremely rosy in the garden, if you'll excuse the pun. But all that seems a long time ago now, a very long time ago.

* * *

When I first clapped eyes on him – Adam, my husband – I don't mind admitting to you I thought he was a bit of all right: perfectly chiselled features, blue eyes, blond hair, lovely high cheekbones – I really thought I was onto a winner. It was as if we'd been especially made for one another. Well, I suppose we had! And at the risk of sounding conceited, I knew that he liked me too. The dead giveaway was his jaw dropping six inches when he first saw me emerge from this mulberry bush. Oh, it was a Kodak moment if ever there was one!

And things were good for a while there; things were very good. We were content just to spend time in each other's company, larking around, playing hide and seek, delighted just to be alive, thankful that God had created us and loved us so much . . . but then things went the shape of a pear.

It amazes me how exuberant, youthful love blinded me so. When I look at Adam now, great lump of lard that he is, those first few days in Eden seem many lifetimes ago. I suppose it's understandable when you think about it – I wasn't exactly spoilt for choice when it came to selecting a partner. Of course where all the trouble really began was with that slippery serpent . . .

* * *

It came slithering up to me one day, oozing silky charm and empty promises, at which point I was convinced it was a male serpent! Normally I'm a pretty sharp cookie, but he must have caught me on a bit of an off-day.

'Ooh!' he says. 'You're not allowed to eat of the fruit. I must say, that's rather mean of God.'

Well, of course I put him straight right away. 'Of course we can,' I says. 'It's just the fruit from that one tree. If we do eat it, or even touch it, we'll die.'

At this point the serpent started making this ridiculous hissing noise, as if to say, 'What are you – daft?'

'That's a lie!' he said, beckoning me closer, as if to share an intimate secret. 'You won't die. God knows that the instant you eat it, you'll become like him. Your eyes will be opened and you will know good from evil. That's the real reason he doesn't want you anywhere near that tree. But remember, you never heard it from me.'

With that he slithered away, back to where he came from.

And I know what you're thinking: you're not going to fall for that one – it's the oldest trick in the book! But be honest: in my position, what would *you* have done?

The fruit looked good. Lovely and fresh, full of ripeness, and it would make me wise. So I took it. And I ate it. And I passed some to Adam, who ate it as well.

Then, for the first time I felt an overwhelming pang of embarrassment. As I stood naked I felt totally self-conscious. Minutes before I hadn't even understood the concept of embarrassment, but now, through the fruit, I had attained that knowledge. And for a brief moment I felt I was on a level playing field with God. Of course, it didn't last.

* * *

He knew. God knew. As if in our wildest imaginations we thought it could be any other way . . .

'Why are you hiding from me, children? Have you eaten from the tree that I warned you about?'

Adam immediately piped up, showing his true colours of grade-A cowardice. 'Yes, we have, but it wasn't my fault – it was her! That woman you lumbered me with, she brought me some and I ate it.' What a pathetic squealer!

Then God spoke to me, asking how I could have done such a terrible thing, and I blamed the serpent, telling him how he had tricked me with his empty promises. But the time of passing the blame was over. I couldn't blame the serpent any more than Adam could blame me. We had to accept the responsibility and the consequences that went with it.

* * *

When people speak of death, they think of the loss of loved ones, and the end of life. For me, death was summed up in our punishment: banishment from Eden. When people read of our fate, I think they imagine us packing our bags and strolling off to another garden a couple of miles down the road, life continuing much as before. How wrong could they be . . .

Our new home is a pale substitute for that garden of perfection. Where we are now is a cold place, dank and dark. There is no happiness, no love . . . no God.

No: for us, things are certainly not so rosy in the garden . . .

Bible reference: Genesis 3

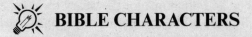 **BIBLE CHARACTERS**

33. The Scarlet Rope

'I live on the edge of society and, ironically, on
the edge of the city, too.'

RAHAB

I know what I am. And I know what people think I am, too! A heathen. A Canaanite, enemy of God's precious people. But, worst of all, a prostitute. Well, why not be frank with you from the very beginning? Officially I'm an innkeeper offering bed and breakfast for the weary traveller, but everyone is well aware of the true nature of my business. I am used to the disgusted looks in the market square, the sly, whispered comments as I pass by, and I suppose over the years I have become immune to them all. Nowadays I just take it in my stride. I live on the edge of society and, ironically, on the edge of the city, too.

My home is built onto the city walls. Two walls to protect our dear Jericho, about 15 feet between them, and my home is built on wooden legs laid across the top of them. From my back window I can look over Jericho; from the front I have a view over the outside wall to the plains of Moab. It's not a very popular location to live, but it suits my business interests perfectly. Mine is the first place a weary traveller comes across, and I can accommodate all requirements.

Recently, though, all travellers have been treated with the utmost suspicion. Talk in the city has all been about an imminent attack by the Israelites, rumours rife about spies infiltrating our walls, finding our weak spots, of which we have many. But for all my failings, I am a born survivor, and I know the smell of defeat – and Jericho reeks of it. I've been thinking for a while about a switch of allegiance. Well, you know the saying – 'If you can't beat 'em, join 'em.' And the opportunity to do that landed right in my lap.

* * *

The visitors arrived, seeking a place to stay for the night, and of course I was more than happy to oblige. Of course it turns out that they were a pair of spies sent over from the Israelite camp in Acacia to see how the land lies. Little did they know our counterintelligence in Jericho is pretty good – about all that is – and our King had been informed of their arrival. So in no time at all the King's crack police squadron arrived to take the spies away for questioning.

In a situation like that, what do you do? What would *you* do? For me, it was decision time. Either I hand them over, stick with my people and probably even get some kind of reward, or I try to cut a deal, start all over again in a new place. For one such as me, the choice was easy.

I took them onto the roof and hid them underneath some piles of flax that were drying. I got rid of the squad by spinning them some terrible yarn about having seen the men but, not realising they were spies, I had let them go. The fools believed me. I told them if they hurried they would probably catch up. So off they went, tripping over each other.

Then I went and spoke to the men, those spies. I told them I knew that their God would deliver my city into their hands. I told them how the people of Jericho were scared to death of their power – the power that parted the Red Sea for Moses, the power that overthrew and destroyed the Amorite kings Sihon and Og. And I begged them, 'If I help you escape, rescue me and my family and their families. Accept us into your community.' And to all my requests they agreed. They gave me a rope to hang from my window and told me that all those in the house decorated with this marker would be rescued, so long as I did not betray them to anyone. For my part I agreed to their conditions. Then, lowering them on a rope from my front window outside the city walls, I sent them to hide in the mountains until the search party was called off.

As they escaped, I hung the rope from my window and laughed to myself when I saw its colour – scarlet!

* * *

Now I wait. All these things happened some three days ago. Early this morning the squad returned, empty-handed, looking fearful and dejected. I hope the spies survive the mountains and have now safely crossed back over the River Jordan. I hope that they have passed on plans of how to conquer this poisoned city. But most of all I hope that in their excitement they don't forget me, and our bargain. The scarlet rope. For all my adult life I have been remembered for my moral failure. Now I want to be remembered for my faith. And so from now on I will wait. By my window I'll wait.

Bible references: Joshua 2:1–24; 6:22–25

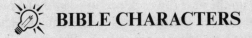 **BIBLE CHARACTERS**

34. The Unwise Career Move

'To understand my rash thinking, you probably
need to be a father. She was a beautiful
twelve-year-old girl; the apple of my eye.'

JAIRUS

I may be the ruler of our synagogue, the big cheese, with all the power to use as I see fit, but in reality even I have my orders. It's the same in all walks of life, I reckon. However high you climb up your particular ladder, there is always someone on the next rung up, peering down on you. For me it was the beloved Pharisees. It's a well-known fact that the synagogues have 'close ties' with the Pharisees; if truth be known, we're pretty much in their pockets.

And this Jesus character had them running about like headless chickens. We were told, in no uncertain terms, not to consort with the so-called King of the Jews in any way, shape or form. To do so would bring harsh consequences. The mere thought of bowing down to him – well, it was unthinkable!

Yet that's what I did. I fell at his feet.

Crazy, you might think; certainly not a wise career move. But as far as the consequences were concerned, I just didn't care. At best, they were of secondary concern.

*   *   *

To understand my rash thinking, you probably need to be a father. She was a beautiful twelve-year-old girl, the apple of my eye.

And my beautiful girl was very sick – sick to the point of death – and I was desperate. I was a respected member of the religious authorities, with the right to commune directly with God and the power to change the course of people's lives, yet I was out of control. There was nothing I could do to help her. Total desperation.

The only person I could think of who could help was this Jesus, the one man I was forbidden to see. But I didn't care. I knew that he was in the Decapolis region, just south-east of the Sea of Galilee, so I set off to see him, determined that he would help in my plight.

When I arrived, there were crowds everywhere. Jesus was undoubtedly a man of the people. And as I made my way over, the crowds recognised me and, out of respect or sheer surprise at my presence, allowed me a direct path through. Before Jesus could say a word I fell to my knees and pleaded with him to heal my little girl. I told him that she was at the very point of death, but I believed that if he could just come and place his hands on her, she would live.

After I had spoken, there followed a surprised hush. And in that quiet, all who were present knew what I had done. The step that I had made. The risk that I had taken. But I didn't care. I was scared no more.

Jesus reached out his hand, helped me to my feet and indicated for me to lead the way to my home. As we set off, the crowd thronged around with gathering impatience, pressing in on us from all sides. I charged forward, pushing people aside, trying to make the path clear for Jesus to walk, aware that time was of the essence. Then, suddenly, for no apparent reason, he stopped.

'Who touched my clothes?' he asked, looking at the crowds. Given the situation, it seemed a ridiculous question. His disciples explained to him the crowds were pushing from all sides, but he was adamant, looking around trying to detect a particular individual.

Shortly afterwards, a woman confessed. She had been suffering from a condition which caused her to bleed constantly, and she thought that if she could just touch his clothing, she would be healed. And, miraculously, she was. Jesus said to her, 'Daughter, your faith has made you well. Go in peace, healed of your disease.' She walked away, tears in her eyes, a transformed woman – an amazing sight for all who witnessed it, except for me.

I felt nothing but frustration. My girl was dying and we were wasting time on a woman with a disease which wasn't even life-threatening! And a disease, incidentally, which forbade her from even having contact with other Jews. I know it sounds selfish, but I only had one thought in my mind.

As I turned to continue pushing through the crowds, I saw, just ahead, one of my servants walking towards me slowly and with a grave countenance. 'It's too late,' he said. 'Trouble Jesus no more: your daughter is dead.' I froze. I didn't feel sadness, or anger at that woman, or frustration at Jesus for not hurrying – I just felt nothing, a void. And then I felt Jesus touch my arm. He looked at me and said, 'Don't worry. Just trust me.' He then beckoned me to continue leading him on.

Before we arrived at my home, the weeping was clearly audible. From well over a hundred yards I could distinguish my wife's voice – groaning and wailing. We went into the bedroom and Jesus announced to all there, 'The child isn't dead, she is only asleep.' Those gathered laughed in bitter derision, but as they did so Jesus cleared the room, leaving just my wife and me with two or three of his followers.

As Jesus took her hand, I remember thinking, 'I know what's going to happen.' He spoke to her gently: 'Get up, little girl.' And she did, immediately. With great energy she jumped out of bed and started walking around, probably wondering what all those people were doing gathered round her bed. My wife began to cry with joy. I did too – not quite to the extent that she did, but tears of joy nevertheless.

Before Jesus left, he told us to keep all these events quiet and also to give the child something to eat. We obeyed him in both matters.

As for me, and my future, I know that I've probably not made the wisest of career moves, biting the hand that feeds – but sometimes it pays to get the important things of life into perspective, don't you think?

Bible reference: Mark 5:21–43

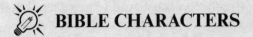 **BIBLE CHARACTERS**

35. Hell Hath No Fury . . .

'Lust is a terrible thing. Oh, at the time it seems wonderful, intoxicating, but in the cold light of day you realise it has the power to destroy.'

MRS POT

I've always been blessed with beauty. Ever since I was a young girl. I can remember, at the age of twelve, realising it for the first time. Noticing that boys and men looked at me in that certain way, their eyes lingering on me a little longer than was strictly necessary. And I knew then that it gave me power over them. A power, I confess, I rather liked, and still do. And I see no reason to apologise for it. In life we all use what we have, whatever it may be. In that sense I am no different from anyone else.

I used my charms to bag a very satisfactory husband, Potiphar, an extremely rich member of Pharaoh's cabinet, well liked and not totally unpleasant to look at, which is always a bonus! We share a sumptuous three-storey house with balconies overlooking lavish gardens. We enjoy the very best in home furnishings, modern arts and haute cuisine, and our social life is an absolute whirl. And as all these delights take place in the upper storeys of our home, on the ground level all the work is done. Not by me, I hasten to add, but by a crack team of servants. And this is exactly where my problems began.

*   *   *

As is the custom, my husband takes the responsibility of the hiring and firing of household staff. Try as I might to get involved with this process it has remained a door securely closed. And to make matters worse, he is not particularly skilled at judging people's character: we've had servants that would rob us blind, butlers that were rude to our esteemed guests, and cooks that didn't know the difference between beef bourguignonne and a Big Mac! But credit where it is due, a few months back Potiphar did find an absolute diamond. His name was Joseph. I saw him around the house from time to time, and he was very pleasing to the eye. And he also had that Midas touch: everything he did was a roaring success – crops flourished, flocks multiplied. He became quite the little favourite with Potiphar. All day long it was 'Joseph did this' and 'Joseph did that'. Well, before too long he was made head of all business affairs, and my husband had not a worry in the world.

* * *

Lust is a terrible thing. Oh, at the time it seems wonderful, intoxicating, but in the cold light of day you realise it has the power to destroy.

I started flirting with Joseph – nothing excessive, just some eyelid-fluttering, a bit of subtle body language. My beauty, my power to attract, had never let me down; in a sense it defined the person I was, the person I am. But the more I tried, the more he just politely ignored me. Surely he couldn't be that innocent? Surely he realised? Surely my powers of attraction weren't deserting me?

Then one day I lost patience with my subtle attempts. I had to resort to more obvious measures. So the first time we were alone I said to Joseph, 'Come, sleep with me.'

Never before had a man rejected my advances, but not only did he refuse me, he seemed horrified at the mere suggestion. 'My master, your husband, trusts me with everything. Everything. He holds nothing back from me except you, because you are his wife. How could I do such a wicked thing? It would be a sin against God!'

I felt disgusting, but I couldn't leave it there. I made a fool of myself, offering myself to him again and again. But his resolve didn't weaken: in fact, it grew stronger. He was obviously a religious fanatic, with his wild talk of sinning against God! But what about disobeying his mistress, the very place where his bread was buttered?

My feeling of self-loathing and rejection grew into one of bitterness and anger. I decided to give him one more chance, and one fateful morning when my husband was out advising

183

Pharaoh on matters of state, I went to Joseph and grabbed him by the sleeve, demanding, 'Sleep with me!' And he said nothing. He wrenched himself away from me and ran, leaving me standing there, his jacket still in my clenched fist. Then I knew. Finally I knew, and I wept.

Hell hath no fury like that of a woman spurned.

I tore at my dress. I screamed for help, and the other servants immediately came running in to help me, to give me the respect I was due. And I told them. I told them the truth: that this Hebrew slave, Joseph, had insulted me. That he had tried to rape me, but when I screamed, he ran – leaving his jacket behind as evidence of his sordid crime. And they comforted me.

And when my husband came home, I told him the truth – this alternative truth which has now become reality. Predictably he was furious, though quite why, I don't know. I am not entirely sure he totally believes me. He has had his beloved Joseph thrown into prison to rot; best thing all round, really.

*   *   *

I've always been blessed with beauty. Ever since I was a young girl. It gives me power over men – a power I confess I rather like. And I see no reason to apologise.

Bible reference: Genesis 39

BIBLE OBSERVERS

36. At the Well

'I don't know anything about living water –
things living in it, maybe!'

WOMAN

Neither of them saw me. Not *him*, sitting down taking a rest by the well. Not *her*, thankfully! Coming to draw her daily water – she didn't see me either.

No, I stayed well hidden. Behind this tree I was, and that suited me just fine. What with him being a Jew, I didn't fancy being scorned. And that woman! Well, to be honest, I just don't mix with her type. I'm sorry, but I do have some standards!

* * *

Anyway, the whole thing happened at about midday, I suppose. Normally I go to draw my water from the well first thing in the morning and then again in the evening. All us girls do – it's a bit of a social gathering, you might say. We share any news, have a bit of a gossip – nothing too vicious, you understand – then off we all go. But this particular morning I'd had a bit of a nightmare. To start with, my husband had had a heavy night on the old grog, so had woken up like a bear with a sore head. On top of that the kids were all larking around, not eating their breakfast, not getting packed for school – so what with all that, I didn't have the time or energy to come to the well. By the time I'd got everyone out of the house and sorted myself out it was the best part of half past eleven.

As I eventually approached the well, who did I see crashed out by the side of the well? None other than this Jewish fella, Jesus. Now, the word on the grapevine is that he's a bit of a one with his teachings and his miracles; some are bowled over by him, others aren't quite so sure. Personally, I didn't really have any opinion. All I needed to know was *I'm* a Samaritan woman, *he's* a Jewish man, so best avoid him. So I hid behind this tree, thinking he'd probably be on his way in a few minutes and then I could carry on. But no, he just sat there.

About ten minutes later who should turn up, rope and bucket in hand, but that woman! I've no idea what her name is, but we girls all used to call her 'the harlot'. It might seem a bit strong, but we had it on very good authority from Betty, who is the fount of all knowledge, that she's been married on numerous occasions.

She always used to come and draw water with the rest of us, first thing in the morning and then again in the evening, but we hadn't seen her for months. Some of the girls used to give her a lot of verbal abuse, so I figure she'd just decided to avoid the busy times – best thing all round, really. Anyway, there she was, walking up to the well, bold as brass, not a care in the world, and this Jesus sitting there, plain for all to see!

So, she just ignores him and starts drawing her water, when all of a sudden he turns and asks her for a drink! Well, you should have seen the look on her face. A Jewish man, lowering himself to speak to a Samaritan woman – it was quite simply unheard of. But she got over the shock and gave him a drink.

Next thing, this Jesus starts telling her something about giving her living water. Well, I don't know anything about living water – things living in it, maybe. But he went on to say this water was a 'perpetual spring within you, watering you for ever with eternal life'. At that point he lost me. I never was the sharpest tool in the box, but she was hanging on to his every word. I don't know how he was going to fetch this special water anyway: he didn't even have a bucket – another one of his miraculous tricks, I've no doubt!

And of course, she was desperate for this everlasting water. Who wouldn't be, if it saved you traipsing up here, day in day out!

Then it got really interesting. Jesus asked her to fetch her husband! That knocked her back a bit – served her right. And she claimed she wasn't married. Ha!

'No,' he says, 'you've had five husbands and you're not

even married to the man you're with now!' Five husbands, I thought to myself – five! Wait till I tell Betty: she'll have a seizure!

I thought fireworks would follow, but he didn't lay into her. A gentle rebuke maybe, but he went on to tell her how we could worship God, Jew and Samaritan alike. That the Messiah will come, and when he did, he would explain everything. Then he told her, 'I am the Messiah.' The promised Messiah.

Just then a bunch of his friends arrived, probably wondering what on earth he was doing chit-chatting with a Samaritan woman. And the harlot, she ran back to the village – even left her bucket and rope in all the rush.

And she told them, 'Come and meet this man, this prophet who knows everything about me. Can it be that he really is the Messiah?'

* * *

And I stayed hidden behind that tree. I was thinking, surely if that harlot is good enough for him, then I must be, too – more than good enough. Because I'm an upstanding and moral woman.

In the end, though, I didn't approach him. Well, he was busy talking to all his friends and shortly afterwards half the village came crowding round him like a flock of sheep. No, I decided to just go back home – and, of course, after all that I didn't even get my water. No water at all.

Bible reference: John 4:1–15

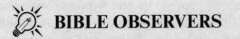 **BIBLE OBSERVERS**

37. The Disappearing Pets

'I've always said, and I've been in the business all
my life, that if you can't trust someone in a pet
shop, where can you trust them?'

SYLVIA

There's no such thing as a nice neighbourhood nowadays!

I know it's a terrible thing to say, and some folk might disagree with me, but sadly it's true.

I mean, you only need to go back a few years and you could leave all your doors and windows wide open without a care in the world. But not now! No, now it's all latchkeys and padlocks and safety chains, even electronic alarms. I ask you! If you'd tried to explain all these safety precautions to my parents' generation, they would have thought you were pulling their leg! But there you are. It's a sign of the times, I suppose, and we had best just get used to it, even if it does make you want to weep.

Take my shop, for instance: Sylvia's Pet Emporium. We've been serving the family pet requirements of the citizens of Jerusalem for three generations now. Of course the business has had its ups and downs: it's had to weather a few plagues and an economic crisis or two, but survived we have and will continue to do. And the reason is, every family loves a pet, and we have something to suit every taste. If it's small you like, we have the very cute fuzzy-tailed Dead Sea gerbils or the gorgeous, flopsy-eared Bethel bunnies. And if it's big you like, we can specially order in cross-eyed camels from the Negev desert. And of course in addition to those we have just about everything in between. Well, I say 'have'; what I should say is 'had', because that is exactly where my problem begins.

*　*　*

Over the past few months I thought I'd noticed a few animals going missing – a chimpanzee here, a parakeet there – but in the end I put it down to my going a bit senile in my old age. I mean, how could the animals go anywhere? They can hardly unlock their cages and just wander off into the sunset, can they? And to even think that anyone might steal them

190

was just beyond my comprehension. That's the beauty of a pet shop, you see; there's something so tranquil and peaceful about them. Well, except all the squawking and squealing of course, but you know what I mean.

Because I've always said, and I've been in the business all my life, that if you can't trust someone in a pet shop, where can you trust them? So, naïvely I just put it to the back of my mind and carried on as usual. Until last week, when I conducted my annual stock check.

Now, normally there's a slight discrepancy – a few bags of feed, maybe, a box of flea collars – and normally it's down to my Arthur not writing clearly in the stockbooks. Admin never was his strong suit. But this time, I couldn't believe what I saw! Dozens of animals were gone. Not just a few – literally dozens. And not just one type either, no! There were fluffy ones, scaly ones, smelly ones, ones that chew the cud, ones that have cloven hoofs – the whole shooting match! The only things untouched were the poor old dodos!

And what was even more mysterious was the quantities that went astray. For every single species that was affected, two went missing. Never one, never three, always two. Work that one out if you can.

And I've been keeping my eyes open, of course, to see if any other pet shops have opened, or zoos – but nothing, not a sign of them. And the amount that's gone missing – well, it would be more than enough to start a new business. It would be more than enough to repopulate the whole earth!

So anyway, against my better principles, I've had to go all security-conscious. We've got chains all over the place, metal bars on the windows, even a security guard on the door. I don't actually call him a security guard: I call it 'pet patrol'. Sounds so much more friendly, don't you think? But it's all so depressing. Still, welcome to the fallen world, Sylvia. Wake up and smell the coffee, my Arthur says.

* * *

191

And as if things weren't bad enough already, I've just noticed it's started to absolutely chuck it down with rain, in the middle of flipping summer, too! Still, at least things can't get any worse, I suppose.

Bible reference: Genesis 6–7

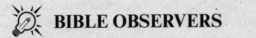 **BIBLE OBSERVERS**

38. When the Band Strikes Up

'I went down to look at the proceedings. It might
sound a bit gruesome, but we don't get much
entertainment round here . . .'

Props

Recording of marching music

MAN

Come on, ladies, gather round and have a close gander at the quality of my produce! I got your apples, your pears, some lovely pineapples and the juiciest little satsumas you'll find anywhere in the Babylonian empire – guaranteed! And I'll tell you what, special offer for you, today only, buy three kilos of any fruit and I'll chuck you in a couple of lovely ripe bananas gratis – can't say fairer than that, can I?

(*Marching band strikes up.*)

Oh, stone the crows, not again! (*Gets on knees*) Oh yes, great King Nebuchadnezzar, we worship you most heartily, blah, blah, blah. (*Music ends.*) Oh, thank goodness! About time too!

That's the new little whim of our beloved King! Every time the band strikes up, we all have to get down on our knees and worship him. I mean, talk about 'the ego has landed'! My poor knees are shot to pieces. Once a day I could cope with, maybe even twice, but every five flipping minutes it's 'bam, diddle, diddle, diddle, bam'. It's enough to drive a sane man completely potty! (*Band strikes up again.*) Oh, you have got to be kidding! (*Music stops. He gets up with visible twinge from his knee.*)

My poor joints! I know what you're thinking: don't do it! Rebel! Refuse to bow down and worship! Who's gonna make you – you're a big burly guy?

And of course the thought of rebellion has occurred to me. But when King Ego came up with this scheme, he also declared a punishment; a statutory, unarguable punishment: anyone failing to bow down and worship would be – wait for it – thrown into a fiery furnace. Not a nice way to go, I think you would agree!

194

Now at first I was a bit doubtful about the sincerity of this particular threat. I mean, I know King Nebbo is a bit of a psycho, but I couldn't envisage even him lobbing a load of his loyal subjects into an industrial furnace. Even so, there was no way I was going to be the first one to blink and test his resolve. I might be tough, but I ain't stupid. Anyway, as it happens, it wasn't long before a few brave volunteers decided to test him out.

* * *

It was three fellers. They all worked in the palace. Can't remember their names – I'll call them Tom, Dick and Harry to keep it simple. Anyway, they got squealed on by some of the King's slimy officials. 'Oh, your Majesty, some of your subjects have defied you, refusing to bow down and worship your gold statue.' Slimeballs!

So, of course, the King hits the roof, his ego temporarily dented, and has these three poor blokes brought up before him.

Now of course, I wasn't there at the time, but word has it that it was the King who blinked first. He gave them one more chance: 'Bow down and worship when the music plays and all will be well.' So the band strikes up – bam, diddle, diddle, diddle, bam – and they just stood there, looking at the King. 'We're not worried about what will happen to us,' they said. 'Throw us into the fire! If it so pleases God he will deliver us. But even if he doesn't, we will never bow down and worship your statue.' Gutsy, eh!

Well, they'd backed the King into a corner, hadn't they? He could hardly withdraw the punishment and show weakness. So, the time was set and the fire was stoked up.

I went down to have a look at the proceedings. It might sound a bit gruesome, but we don't get much entertainment round here – just a few stonings and floggings, the occasional Andrew Lloyd-Webber musical down at the colosseum. But this spectacle was staggering. I was stood a good 100 metres back, but I could feel the heat as if I was right next to it. Tom, Dick and Harry were tied up and thrown into the flames, and as the guards threw them in, the heat and the flames consumed them instantly. And then in the flames I could make out the shadows of men. I counted four – no idea who the other one was! And then the King, in fear and awe, called for Tom, Dick and Harry to come out.

And they did. Not a single burn between them, not a hair singed, a garment destroyed – not even a whiff of smoke! So the King commended their bravery and proclaimed that indeed their God was a good God, worthy of worship. And his permission to do so was truly granted.

*   *   *

I confess, I was impressed! This God that they speak of is a God I would like to know. And the more I find out, the more I research, the more I am impressed at this God of the Jews. To be honest, I'm not sure I'd be prepared to walk into a fiery furnace yet, but one step at a time and we'll see what happens.

As for the King, word has it that he's starting to lose his marbles. I certainly think he's missed the point of true worship. After all he's witnessed, what he himself has confessed, he still sets himself up as worthy of worship. I suppose that's the problem with power: absolute power corrupts absolutely.

Still, maybe one day he'll understand. (*Band strikes up.*) Or maybe not . . .

Bible reference: Daniel 3

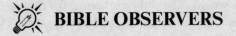 **BIBLE OBSERVERS**

39. The Best Man's Speech

'I tell you, when you open up that boy's cupboard
there's a fair few skeletons rattling about . . . '

GARY

I'm a really laid-back, chilled-out guy – you know what I mean! Everybody says so. 'Gaz,' they say. 'Gaz, you are one seriously chilled-out guy.' And they're right, 'cos nothing ruffles my feathers. I take life as it comes, in my stride, not a care in the world. The only problem with that is, on the rare occasion when you do blow, you blow big-time. And I don't mind admitting to you, the other week I got well annoyed!

It all happened at my best mate's wedding. He's called Colin, and his wife is Marcia, and my job for the day was best man. Now, the wedding was in the pokey little village called Cana in Galilee, where Marcia's parents live – bit of a dump, but at least it was a change of scenery! And the whole thing was going an absolute treat. Colin managed to stay reasonably sober the night before the wedding, and on the actual day me and him looked the absolute bee's knees in our toppers and tails. Marcia didn't look bad, either, in her puffy dress – if you like that sort of thing.

Anyway, the vows went well, nobody muffed their lines, the priest was on form, the guests were all having a great time and on the whole it appeared that nothing could possibly go wrong.

And so began the reception. There were prawn and mushroom vol-au-vents a-plenty. Colin and Marcia were doing the rounds, working the guests like a pair of pros, and most importantly the wine was flowing! Aunty Dotty went a bit overboard on the old Lambrusco and ended up looking a bit silly doing a one-woman rendition of 'YMCA'. But nobody really cared, they were all having an absolute whale of a time – until disaster struck.

* * *

We were just approaching the highlight of the day – the speeches, in particular mine of course – and it promised to be a classic. I had it planned to perfection. I had some lovely new gags, plus a few of the old classics – my opening gambit was going to be, 'Ladies and gentlemen. Unaccustomed to public speaking as I am . . .' Not bad, eh? Anyway, I was really looking forward to winding Colin up. I tell you, when you open up that boy's cupboard there's a fair few skeletons rattling about, and I was prepared to dish the dirt.

But just as I was about to get going, word came through. Disaster. The wine had totally run out. Nothing left, not even a cheapo case from last month's trip to France on the ferry. Nothing to toast the couple, and of course the guests were somewhat disgruntled.

Well, the timing couldn't have been worse. There was me, speech in hand, ready to knock 'em dead, and all anybody cared about was where their next glass of plonk was coming from. It can't get any worse, I thought. Then, of course, it got worse.

Word started circulating there was a miracle man in the house. The son of one of the guests, some woman that Marcia's mum knew from her embroidery group or something. Anyway, he was a bit reluctant, but eventually he offered to help before things started to turn nasty.

Now, in the corner of this room there were six great big stone water pots, each of them with the capacity of a good, oooh, 20 or 30 litres. He told the servants to fill them to the brim with water, which they did post haste.

Now this is where it gets a bit weird. Immediately he got one of the servants, some spotty little local kid, to draw a glass from the water pot and hand it to the father of the bride. There was no time to swap the pots or for any sleight of hand. Believe me – I was watching. Then Marcia's dad received the glass, took a sip and his face lit up. There was a short pause before he declared to the crowd, 'This is wonderful! Best wine of the evening.' The crowd cheered. The band struck up and once more the party went into full swing. A miracle. An undeniable miracle.

'So what's your problem?' you're probably asking. Disaster averted, all things back to normal. Well, not quite! Once the guests got a taste of this wine, they couldn't get enough of it, could they? They all crowded round this Jesus to tell him what a great bloke he was, and all of a sudden *he* became the centre of attention. And I'm the best man! *I'm* supposed to be the centre of attention, but no one was interested in me or my well-prepared, perfectly formed 20-minute speech.

And that's why I'm annoyed – Gaz, the laid-back, chilled-out guy, lost it! Shame, really. I had some great gags, all gone to waste now, of course. I had this classic one about a syringe full of general anaesthetic and a pair of underpants, but it'll never see the light of day. Shame.

And this Jesus, the miracle man who stole my moment of glory – apparently he left the wedding early and went up to Capernaum with his mum and brothers and mates, probably to open a cut-price wine merchant's or something.

And the more I think about him, the more he fascinates me. If I can get beyond my anger I'd love to see him and ask him how he did it. Just exactly how he did it.

Bible reference: John 2

☀ BIBLE OBSERVERS

40. The Missing Picnic

'Little did we realise at the time that this was
going to be the strangest picnic we'd ever
been on!'

MARION

I shouldn't say this really, 'cos I know it'll make me sound like a really heartless mother, but in my opinion school summer holidays are a complete living nightmare. Weeks and weeks of nothingness lie ahead, with your moody off-spring constantly carping away. 'What are we doing today? Mum, can we go and do such-and-such? I'm bored!' It's enough to drive you totally doolally. I mean, I'm as creative as the next person, but there's only so many ideas you can come up with to keep them occupied.

One thing we do all enjoy, and we make a point of doing it every holiday, is to go on a nice picnic. Admittedly, there's not much to a picnic. It's easy enough to organise, and very cheap, but somehow it feels like a real treat. We've got a spot we always go to. Takes about an hour to walk there, but it's well worth the trip. It's a lovely secluded spot on the shores of the Sea of Galilee, very close to Bethsaida. The sea's always calm and you get some lovely views, plus of course plenty of space for the kids to run and lark about. There's also a little inlet, with a couple of stalls selling Mr Whippy icecreams and kosher burgers. Totally overpriced, so we don't bother!

Anyway, we raided the kitchen and the local shop for some picnic treats. I must admit we do go a bit over the top. Ginsters pasties, those Dairylea cheesy things, egg sand-wiches, bacon frazzles, cheese footballs, even a box of fondant fancies – our particular favourite. We all loaded up our bags and off we went. Little did we realise at the time that this was going to be the strangest picnic we'd ever been on.

For starters, when we arrived at our 'secluded' spot it was totally chocka. Literally thousands of people all cluttering up the beach and sprawled over the banks of the river. Don't get me wrong: I wasn't expecting to have the whole place to ourselves, but this was ridiculous! I've always had a bit of a thing about my own personal space, and it was all we could do to find a few square feet to park ourselves. And the family that were next to us – well, I'm no snob, but they were absolutely revolting. They had the manners of a herd of pigs – and the language! Well, I can't bring myself to repeat it.

Shortly afterwards we found out that all the hoo-ha was because this so-called miracle man called Jesus was somewhere around, and he was due to give a bit of a talk and do some healings. Well, I thought, it could work out nicely – he can have a look at me and see if he can sort out my weak ankles, which, incidentally, are the bane of my life. Of course he never got round to me, but that was the least of my worries. Things were about to get even more problematic.

Impatient as ever, my two started belly-aching that they were hungry, so I suggested we unpack the bags and start the picnic. I'd brought all the boring stuff – the blanket, plates, cups, cutlery etc – and the kids had the food. I watched them unpack their bags with growing despair. They'd brought everything you could imagine – gameboys, magazines, Harry Potter books, buckets and spades – you name it! Everything except the food.

'We thought you were bringing the food, Mum!' they both whined. Even after I'd specifically given them that task. So the three of us sat there like a bunch of lemons, surrounded by piles of toys and empty plates.

Not the most successful picnic, I think you'd agree. No room to move and no food to eat – even the kosher burger man was apparently having the day off. And it was at this point that things went from the problematic to the downright strange.

* * *

This Jesus fellow was in mid-flow, but time was knocking on and there were a lot of hungry people apparently also without a picnic. Jesus's gang of sidekicks were wanting the crowds to disperse to go home for their tea. But Jesus had a different idea. 'We should feed them,' he says. 'Gather together what food you can.'

So a short while later they came back to him with what they'd rustled up: five tiny little loaves of Hovis and a couple of scrawny-looking fish. Not much of a feast, I thought. The yobbish-looking family next to us would have happily polished off the lot and still been hungry.

But with that, Jesus looked up to the sky, prayed a prayer and started breaking the bread. And as he did so it was never-ending. He got the disciples to help him, and the same thing happened. However much they broke off, the bread seemed to be everlasting. So we all ate. Picnic or no picnic, we all ate. And we ate till we were full. I was awestruck – totally mystified by what was happening, but awestruck. The kids didn't seem overly impressed. As soon as they'd finished their food, they started playing with the gameboys and reading magazines. But I knew I'd witnessed something out of this world.

* * *

When we got home a few hours later, my husband was back and I told him all that had happened; everything from the vast crowds to the forgotten picnic and the miraculous feeding. He looked a little bit dubious about some things, understandably I suppose, but he was happy enough. Well, why wouldn't he be? It's not often he gets a fondant fancy with his supper . . .

Bible reference: Luke 9:10–17

☀ BIBLE OBSERVERS

41. Concubine Number 299

'I might as well go around wearing a t-shirt
saying, "Only to be used in case of an
emergency!"'

SAMANTHA

You may think I have the life of old Riley, me, but let me tell you something: you'd be wrong. More wrong than you could ever imagine. I work for his Majesty, the oh-so-noble King Solomon, but before I go on I'll admit to you I'm no longer one of his most important or influential employees.

You've probably heard all the gossip that he's got 700 wives and 300 concubines – well, I can exclusively reveal it's all true. Most blokes complain about having one wife, but Solomon's obviously a bit of a glutton for punishment! And how do I know the inside track from the palace, you might ask? Well, because I'm one of them. Not a wife, a concubine. To be absolutely precise, concubine number 299!

Bearing in mind there's only 300 of us, I'm sure you can understand that, when it comes to the pecking order around here, I don't really get much of a look-in. For starters, the wives get the best treatment, and there's 700 of them to cater for now. When I first got a job here, he only had about a dozen wives. At that time he had slightly higher standards. But now he marries anything that moves!

It's strictly forbidden in our faith for him to marry a woman from a foreign nation, but he flagrantly disregards that now. If it will ease foreign relations or help in trade negotiations, he's there, more than happy to make a compromise. So we've now got wives cluttering up the place – you can't swing a dead cat around without hitting another wife. And they've all got their peculiar quirks and idols to worship. It's slowly eroding the faith we used to so admire the King for.

So, that's the wives. Now, next down the line are we concubines. Not so important as the wives maybe, bit of a weak salary-and-benefits package, but we're there to serve the King whenever he needs us. And for certain girls there are some quite nice perks. Take concubine number 1, for instance: a dark, ravishing beauty from Samaria, without doubt the King's current personal favourite. Well, it's all right for her, this job: she gets the lot – jewels such as you've never seen, great platters of grapes and other luscious fruits on tap, Dolce and Gabbano outfits – you name it. And as long as you're fairly high up the tree, there's always a few little perks going.

But by the time it gets to number 299, you can imagine there's not a lot of luxuries left. I might as well go round wearing a t-shirt saying, 'Only to be used in case of an emergency!' I did get something last week though: an out-of-date Snickers bar, it was. Not much, but better than nothing, I suppose.

And of course I know all about how it works, because I used to be up there myself, in my glamorous youth. Number 12 was the loftiest position I reached when I was at the absolute peak of my powers. Still, no use dwelling on the past, is there? It'll just turn you bitter, like lots of the girls here. The bitching and gossiping that goes on is beyond belief. I don't bother any more. Mind you, what he sees in concubine number 7 I'll never know: she's got a face like the back end of a chariot.

* * *

No, you don't work as long as I have without noticing a few things. Sad, really, to watch how the mighty fall. In his prime, old Solomon was a force to be reckoned with. With his incredible gift of wisdom he ruled effectively and was sought out by rulers across the world. Now all he cares about is building loads of temples and palaces encrusted with gold and ivory, and taxing his own people to the hilt, working them into the ground.

His own people, who so loved him, have started to despise him, while outsiders still revere him! They still come from far and wide to experience his incredible wisdom. And he still is wise, in his own way. More wisdom than he knows what to do with, wisdom coming out of his ears. No common sense, of course, but that's a different thing.

* * *

Recently I think he started to seriously lose the plot, just in the past few weeks. The other day I saw him pacing up and down the corridors, flailing his arms all over the place crying, 'Meaningless, meaningless, life is utterly meaningless!' Tell me about it, I thought. I could have told you that years ago without the supernatural gift of wisdom. Imagine the life I've had! I shouldn't think you could dream up something that more closely epitomises a meaningless life. Still, I'm not complaining. I've got a roof over my head, and what more can a fading beauty such as I ask for?

And if the King thinks it's all meaningless, with all his wisdom and faith and riches – well, what hope is there for the rest of us?

* * *

King Solomon. Among the many nations there was no king like him. He was loved by his God, and God made him king over all Israel. But even he was led into sin, and by foreign women.

Work that one out, if you can.

Bible reference: 1 Kings 11

☀ BIBLE OBSERVERS

42. A Guppy's View

'We hip and trendy guppies pull all the birds.
Well, obviously not birds – we don't go in for
those cross-species relationships.'

GRAHAM

Well, I've had a good life. There's no getting away from it: life has been good.

Some might say my life has been rather insignificant. Or, put another way, 'There's plenty more fish in the sea.' And I confess that's exactly what I am. One of the millions of guppies born, bred and raised in the Sea of Galilee. You might laugh, you might think it a rather boring life – but, boy, have we had some laughs!

* * *

For instance, have a guess what my favourite hobby is. Swimming! Well, to be honest it's my only hobby, but I'm really good at it. And of course, when you live in the sea you need to be, 'cos you might not know this, but the sea is an incredibly perilous place to live. Everywhere you turn there's danger, and you had better get wise to it, and fast.

For starters, I think you'll agree we guppies are incredibly sleek and attractive specimens. But it's not the same for all the creatures that live down here. Without wishing to appear rude, some breeds are downright ugly. Some have these big, horribly bulbous eyes, others have great big rubbery lips, some even have disgusting spikey things sticking out all over the place – ugh, it's vile! So of course they get a bit jealous, 'cos we hip and trendy guppies pull all the birds. Well, obviously not birds – we don't go in for those cross-species relationships – but we pull all the fit fish – you get my drift!

But then if it's not some jealous, ugly breed chasing after you, the biggest threat of all is from above – the nets that descend from the sky. Every now and then they appear on the surface of the water – great bell-shaped nets, with lead weights around the edge, slowly sinking towards you, and you have to shift double quick. If you don't, there's a sharp tug of a cord and you are drawn upwards, never to be seen again. It's another peril of living in the sea, and I've lost numerous kith and kin to this danger. We all live our lives with one eye permanently looking up for the nets.

Of course, the real enemy isn't the net itself – that's just a tool – it's the one that throws the net you have to blame. And the greatest nemesis of the guppy clan is this big hairy hulk of a bloke called Simon Peter. Pretty much every day he's on the prowl, casting his nets in the hope of sweeping up great hordes of my family and friends. But during our lifetime we've got wise to his methods. And on this particular day we had the better of him and no mistake.

We would all gather together in a big bunch, and he would heave his great net over the side of the boat. Then, quick as we could, we would dash under his boat and regroup on the other side. Oh, we all laughed! And old Simon Peter, who had a right fierce temper, would gather up his net, totally empty, cursing like a Trojan, then throw it over the other side. But of course, as soon as he did that, we would all dive back under the boat, back to where we were in the first place. I looked through the surface of the water, and old Simon Peter was hopping mad, stomping around the boat like a man possessed.

Now, you might think that after a couple of times of to-ing and fro-ing this game would get a bit on the boring side, but nothing of the sort – we kept it going all day, back and forth, and had more fun than any guppy could hope for or deserve.

But it was just then, at the moment of our greatest confidence, that things began to go rather wrong. Another bloke appeared, an apprentice of Simon Peter, we thought, and the tide began to turn. We were all gathered on one side of the boat and, just as Simon Peter prepared to cast his nets towards us, this other bloke tells him to try the other side – pretty pointless, you might think, 'cos there was nothing there. Simon Peter reluctantly agreed, and the net once more splashed onto the water and slowly began to sink.

For what happened next there is no logical explanation.

My mind told me to just stay put and all would be well, but my body, as if by some inexplicable force, drew me into the span of the net. Try as I might to avoid its terrifying reach I was helpless, caught in its power. The cord was pulled tight and we were all caught, every last one of us, drawn out of the water for the last time, never to be seen again.

* * *

And now here I am, lying in this bucket at Harry Ramsden's. Lends a whole new meaning to the word 'gutted'. Any minute now I'll be dipped in batter and then ceremoniously dropped into boiling hot oil – not a very nice end to this story, is it really? But there is hope for my species. You see, we were the last victims. From now on we're not the target – you are! That's got you worried, hasn't it! You see, this other bloke, the one we thought was Simon Peter's apprentice, I heard his last words. And he said, 'From now on you'll be fishing for the souls of men.'

How do you feel about that, humans? The guppy clan is safe to flourish, but you lot – well, I'm not so sure. He's after the souls of men, you included. And, believe me, he's good.

It's about to end for me now. No complaints, I suppose. But with my last breath I'll give you this warning – watch out! Keep one eye permanently looking up for the nets . . .

Bible reference: Luke 5

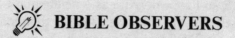 **BIBLE OBSERVERS**

43. The Tolerant Neighbour

'There comes a time when you have to draw a
line. A line which, out of respect, should not be
crossed. Last week my neighbour crossed
that line.'

NEIGHBOUR

I'm a tolerant person, and don't let anyone tell you any different. I don't get upset by every tiny little thing and expect things to be just so all the time. My very nature is to give people a bit of leeway, allow them a bit of room to manoeuvre, so to speak. And as a neighbour, even if I do say it myself, I think I am very fair. If there's a bit of an early morning DIY session going on, even on a Sunday, I'm not even slightly perturbed. A party going on till the wee small hours, I don't even bat an eyelid – all the best to them, I say. You've got to let your hair down once in a while after all.

And I can tell you, I've had my fair share of odd neighbours. This one woman in my home town has a strange obsession with Barbara Streisand. For two hours every morning she'd have her screeching away at top volume while she did her housework, and I never complained once. Another guy, when I lived just the other side of Capernaum, had a funny thing about shelves. Every other day he was banging and tapping, erecting yet another wonky effort, and yet, friends, I never said a word. Each to their own. As I said to you, I am a very tolerant person.

But there comes a time, I think you'll agree, when you have to draw a line. A line which, out of respect, should not be crossed.

Last week my neighbour crossed that line.

* * *

It was a Wednesday, I remember, 'cos I was just coming home from my weekly line dancing, looking a bit of a prune in my cowboy boots and ten-gallon hat. I turned into our little cul-de-sac, and all I can say is my jaw dropped. Normally, it's a very quiet and secluded area, the very reason I purchased it in the first place. But this particular evening it looked more like the flipping Mardi Gras. There were people everywhere, strewn all over the street, chatting and laughing – and it was all centred around the house of my next door neighbour.

I pushed my way through the crowds to get to my front door, went inside, took off my hat and boots and put on the kettle. As I sat with my feet up, enjoying a nice, relaxing cup of herbal tea, I decided to let it go. So the neighbours were having a party which got a bit out of hand – a few too many uninvited guests. It happens. And then, glowing in the pride of my liberal tolerance, I even treated myself to a chocolate hobnob. But just as I had my first bite things took a bit of a turn.

The banging started. Not a normal banging, but one that literally shook the foundations of the house. I thought the roof was going to cave in. This is ridiculous, I thought, so out I went, sharpish, to investigate. The crowds were still all milling around, but there on the roof was a group of vandals, banging away like mad things.

I scooted up the outside stairway onto the flat roof to confront them. 'Oi,' I said. 'What do you think you're playing at? This isn't *Changing Rooms*, you know!'

They all looked at me, petrified, and one of them replied, 'Please, we're just trying to help him.' The four vandals pointed to a fifth man: a cripple, paralysed from birth apparently, lying awkwardly on this dodgy-looking home-made stretcher. 'That man in there can help him.'

By this time they'd carved out a great hole in the roof, big enough for a man to go through. And their plan was to lower the man in on the stretcher, thus bypassing all the milling crowds. I said to them it sounded a bit dangerous – he could fall off. But, looking at this poor guy, I decided he didn't have a lot to lose. So down he went, lowered using a rather primitive pulley system, but successful all the same. And we all peered in through the hole to see what this healer would make of it all.

He looked at this guy lying on the stretcher, whose face

was a mixture of agony and hope and belief. And the healer simply said, 'Son, your sins are forgiven.'

Well, the place went into uproar! Among the crowd were some of the leaders of the Jewish religion, and they were heckling, 'Who do you think you are?' 'That's blasphemy!' 'Only God can forgive sin.' But the healer didn't back down. No, quite the opposite, he squared up to them.

'Fair point,' he said. 'Anyone can say, "Your sins are forgiven." Talk is cheap; you want proof.' And with that, he turned to the paralysed man and commanded him, 'Get up. Pick up your stretcher and go home. You are healed.' And he did. There was no dramatic pause, with the crowd all waiting with baited breath. Immediately the guy jumped up, picked up his stretcher and pushed through the crowds. Unbelievable. His friends were on their feet cheering and dancing about. I must admit I joined in the celebrations too – very nearly fell down the hole in the roof!

'We've never seen anything like this before,' they cried. And neither had I.

* * *

Which brings me back to my complaint with my dear neighbour. If he's going to host parties like that in the near future, and with guests like that holding court, then as his neighbour I should be invited and given front-row seats. I would have thought it was the least I could expect, being such a tolerant person.

Bible reference: Mark 2:1–12

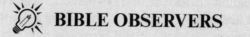

BIBLE OBSERVERS

44. The Fatted Calf

'I don't mean to sound all superior or cocky, but I
really have managed to land on my hoofs.'

Someone up there must like me. I don't mean to sound all superior or cocky, but I really have managed to land on my hoofs. Take all the other calves here on the estate: skinny little runts, they are. Moping around, making these horrible little bleating noises. (*Bleats*) It's pathetic. Then look at me. Treated like royalty, I am. I've got my own penthouse pen, with an ensuite bathroom and breakfast bar – the works!

And the food they give me! Well, anybody would think they were trying to fatten me up on purpose. I get absolutely piles of the stuff. Left-over meat, potatoes, vegetables, fruit, gallons of milk, tubes of Pringles, bags of peanut M&Ms, you name it. I'll be honest with you, I'm building up a little bit of a paunch. Still, who's complaining? Whether things are going well for the Master or not, he always makes sure I'm fed well, and recently, I'm sad to report, he has been in for a bit of a personal trial.

It's all the fault of his youngest son. A precocious little brat if ever there was one. I never liked him or his constant whining. Anyway, as if his father wasn't generous enough, the cheeky little tyke asked for his inheritance early. Fair enough, if the Master had offered him an advance, but no, he just comes out and asks for it. As good as spitting in his father's face, in my opinion.

So, the Master, being the country gentleman that he is, gives the little brat his share, and off he goes. Things then carried on as usual at the estate – the brat hardly raised a finger to help with anything, so he wasn't really missed. The only thing that noticeably changed was the Master. He'd always been so upbeat and cheerful. But now he became much less animated, looking like he was carrying the weight of the world on his shoulders. It was very sad to see.

We got regular reports of the brat's activities. There's always someone somewhere anxious to pass on a bit of gossip. And all the reports were tales of the highlife – fast cars, fast women, booze and bingeing, late-night clubbing every night, gambling – oh, he was having a right old time by the sound of it.

Then, as tends to happen with Lady Luck, things took a turn for the worse. The money ran out. The fast cars were sold to pay off his debts. The fast women sped off even quicker than they'd arrived, and the brat was all alone: an inexperienced little boy without a penny to his name, all alone in the big wide world.

The reports continued to come through of his hopeless wanderings. There was talk he got work as a farmhand feeding pigs. Imagine a young Jewish lad feeding pigs! One report even suggested that in total desperation and hunger he dropped to his hands and knees and started eating the same slops as the pigs. Personally, I find that one hard to believe: the pig is a ceremonially unclean animal, totally defiled. To even touch one is a no-go area, let alone dine with one. But needs must, I suppose. If I had a bit more heart I'd feel sorry for him, but after the way he behaved towards his father I reckon he was only getting what he deserved. As did his older brother.

Then, one day, no surprise, he comes back, tail between his legs, to ask for his father's forgiveness. The barefaced cheek of it! I was willing the Master to tell him to get lost, but it just isn't in his nature. No, when he heard his son was to return, the depression that had hung over him like a cloud immediately lifted. As soon as the brat appeared, his father ran to him. A man of his stature normally walks very slowly, but so delighted was he to see his boy, he hitched up the hem of his garment above his knees and sprinted towards him. For the sentimental among you, I suppose it was a lovely moment.

The older son, though, was not happy, and understandably so. He'd been working his backside off, loyal to his father all that time, and his loser of a brother was returned to his original position, all misdemeanours forgiven and forgotten. He complained to his father, told him how he felt.

And his father told him, 'You and I are close. Everything that I have is yours. But we should celebrate. He is your brother, who was dead and who has come back to life. He was lost and is found.' And you can't argue with that, I suppose.

What makes matters even worse is the father's plan for a welcome-home celebration. A veritable feast. Apparently it's going to be huge. Everyone's invited: his extended family, local dignitaries, friends and staff of the estate – there'll be hundreds of guests. I tell you, he is going to need to slaughter a herd of those scrawny animals to feed them all. I don't know where he is going to get them from. Still, I'm sure he'll sort something out. Unless, of course . . . No, he wouldn't, would he? . . . Would he?

Bible reference: Luke 15:11–32

CONTEMPORARY

45. The Vanishing Princess

'She slowly became this walking skeleton, her
bones visible . . .'

PAULA

I'm no expert, but if you ask me it all started for her back at school, primary school even. She was never part of the in-crowd – you know, that snooty group of girls with gaggles of boys following their every move. No, she was never one of them, but she had a nice little group of friends, you know, just . . . well, nice. Anyway, the other kids decided to nickname her – porky pig. Porky pig.

Now, I know as a mother I'm probably somewhat biased, but really, by no stretch of the imagination could you call her fat or porky. Don't get me wrong – she wasn't skinny, then. No, just, well, you know, normal. But you know kids. They never let up, do they? So porky pig it remained.

We knew it upset her a bit, but Richard and I used to make light of it. 'Oh, just ignore them,' we would say. 'If they see it doesn't bother you, they'll soon get bored and leave you alone.' But that was the problem. It did bother her, and kids have got an uncanny ability to know just when they're hitting the spot.

It continued all through primary school. We didn't particularly know at the time. I mean, how could we? She never said anything. Looking back now, though, I can see the effect. She was always the life and soul . . . but slowly that all disappeared. She became a loner, so introverted; it was all Richard could do to get her to smile! Neither of us could understand what was happening – what was happening to our little princess.

* * *

I think part of her was relieved to be leaving primary school, which she of course saw as a place of daily torture; but the other part was filled with dread at moving to grown-up school. I dropped her off on the first morning – ashen-faced, she was. I didn't think too much of it. 'Of course she's nervous,' I thought. 'Everybody is on their first day at a new school.' At home things remained the same. She was quiet, moody. But at school, as we were to find out later, things had taken a cruel turn.

The porky pig nickname had obviously run its course. It was probably seen as a bit tame for her youthful tormentors. The same mistake could not be made with her new title: fat cow. Fat cow. *Fat cow.* What can drive one human being to call another human being such a terrible thing? Week in, week out, day after day, hour after hour: *fat cow, fat cow, fat cow!*

We knew nothing about it. If we had, Richard and I would have been straight up to the school to see the head. I could see she was unhappy, though. I should have forced her to tell me why, gone up to see the teachers anyway, but you don't, do you? You just let it go on and on.

* * *

It was in that first year at senior school that she started on the dieting. At first I thought it was just a fad – you know, one of those things teenagers go through, nothing to worry about. But as the weeks and months went on it got progressively serious, to the point where she was hardly eating anything at all. Dry toast, a few vegetables, a bit of fruit if you were lucky. It all had the desired effect, though. The weight literally fell off her, stone after stone. Richard hadn't got a clue what was going on. 'Ah, get a few burgers and fry-ups down her – she'll be as good as new.' It's not that he didn't care – he just didn't understand.

She slowly became this walking skeleton, her bones visible. We started on the endless rounds of doctors, dietitians and specialists, but I don't know if they do any good. Richard never speaks about it. Typical man, keeping it all huddled in, but I know from time to time he cries. On his own, in the bedroom. I've heard him. I don't go in, though. He needs to keep his steel exterior intact. But I know it breaks his heart to see his little princess vanishing.

I've been doing a bit of research. I was never much of a scholar, I admit, but it's been really interesting. Lots of stuff about eating disorders, anorexia, bulimia. I thought I had to do something. I just felt so helpless, my daughter vanishing before my eyes, and me not knowing what to do. Of course, these books explain how all the professional help can work, but they also say that many victims overcome their problem through the support and love of family and friends.

Now, I don't understand most of that stuff. It's all much too brainy for me. But I've got this belief that all the lies she was told – the porky pig, the fat cow, the waste of space – I have the power to drown out, by telling her over and over the truth as it is, as I see it. That she's fearfully and wonderfully made. That she is beautiful. That she is precious. That she is worth so much and has so much to live for.

Oh God, I don't want much, maybe I don't deserve much, but please don't take my child from me! I can weather a storm like anyone else, but I don't think I could cope if I were to outlive my child, my only child, my princess.

Bible reference: Proverbs 12:18

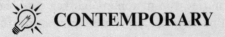 **CONTEMPORARY**

46. Never Satisfied

'It's all right for some, isn't it, being able to drop
the best part of £1,000, just like that, on a
television set?'

MAUREEN

Personally I don't think it's fair that we always have to go round to hers. I mean, at the end of the day I am her older sister, and as such I think my opinion should count for something. She's done all right for herself, though, our Elizabeth. Married Charles, the merchant banker, and they live in a lovely postmodernistic converted farmhouse on the outskirts of town.

Don't get me wrong, though: I'm not envious or anything, no! It wouldn't be any good for us, anyhow. Too much of that fresh country air plays havoc with my Arthur's sinus condition – one whiff of cow dung and he's all bunged up for a fortnight!

'Maureen,' she says to me, 'Charles and I are only too happy to jump in the BMW and come over to see you. We just thought you and Arthur might be more comfortable coming over to us. I can knock us up a lovely non-spicy something in the Aga, and then we can all eat out on the patio al fresco!' Al fresco – I ask you! 'And if Arthur wants a few cans of stout, you can always stay over in one of our six spare bedrooms.' Flippin' cheek! She jolly well knows Arthur's been off the stout for 18 months under doctor's orders due to his dodgy ticker.

Arthur's always been one for the easy life, though, so we go over there just to keep the peace, and Liz gleefully shows us around all their new rooms and extensions.

Don't get me wrong, though: I'm not envious or anything, no! I'm very happy with our ex-council-owned two-up two-down with its creaky staircase and outside loo. I mean, it's a roof over your head, and that's all you need, isn't it? Mind you, it could do with a lick of paint, especially on the landing. There's not much chance of getting my Arthur up on a ladder nowadays, not after his quadruple hernia op!

* * *

She phoned me up the other week, just before Wimbledon fortnight, all excited. 'Oh Maureen, you'll never guess what we've just bought!' A small country, for all I know, I thought to myself, but I didn't say it out loud. 'A brand new Nicam stereo, Dolby surround, 3-D phonic widescreen television! Charlie's going to set up an extension lead so I can watch Wimbledon al fresco on the veranda with champagne, strawberries and cream!' It's all right for some, isn't it, being able to drop the best part of £1,000 just like that on a television set?

Don't get me wrong, though: I'm not envious or anything, no! I'm perfectly happy with our Radio Rentals £49.99 ex-rental antique. Although I wouldn't say no to a remote control. Not for me, you understand – it's just not very good for Arthur getting up every five minutes to change the channel, not with his weak ankles.

I honestly don't know why I fork out for a TV licence anyway. I mean, there's nothing on, is there, except a load of old repeats? To be frank, I don't watch a thing. Well, except the soaps, and a bit of sport – I do like my snooker. But apart from that, there's nothing! Although I'm not averse to a good murder mystery. Not all of them – my preference is for Morse or Frost. Well, they don't graphically show the murders, do they? My Arthur always insists on the news. I find it so depressing. Still, I suppose you need to keep up with the current issues, don't you?

* * *

The other thing Liz is getting all excited about is her upcoming hols. Apparently Saint Charles has booked them three weeks cruising around the Caribbean on some luxury liner, followed by a couple of weeks' pampering at a five-star hotel. How simply smashing!

Don't get me wrong, though: I'm not envious or anything, no! I'm perfectly happy with two weeks at our usual holiday home in Camber Sands, complete with its leaking roof and psychotic maid. And anyway, it would be impossible for us to fly anywhere nowadays. Arthur's knees blow up like balloons if he goes above 10,000 feet; apparently it's water retention or some such thing.

Anyhow, I'm sure Liz and Charles will have an absolute ball! She'll come back wearing a grin like a Cheshire cat, and with all that sun will no doubt be the colour of . . . well, the colour of a foreign person. And I'll tell you something else: she'll still want to go somewhere different, do something new, buy something else. You see, that's the problem with rich people: they're never flipping satisfied . . .

Bible reference: Proverbs 14:30

47. Never Never Land

'The lure of something-for-nothing or shortcut
ways to live beyond my means has never lost its
attraction.'

JOHN

It's taken me years to admit it, but looking back now I reckon that sometimes, just maybe, I should have listened to my old dad. He was a daft old duffer, no mistake, and most of his so-called advice was, well, vaguely ludicrous. For instance, his prehistoric opinion on how a man should treat his woman was so frighteningly non-PC that to speak it aloud in our enlightened times would very probably herald prosecution and an immediate lynch mob! But on the odd occasion, very seldom I admit, he would come out with an absolute gem.

Now, one of his overlooked classics, and I can hear him say the words now as if it were yesterday, was this: 'Never pay on the never-never. If you can't afford it, you can't have it.' Not startlingly original advice, I admit. Thousands of conservative parents have echoed this advice throughout the decades to errant and irresponsible offspring. But when I first heard these words of wisdom I was probably only about eleven or twelve, and the notion of being able to own something and never have to pay for it, well, it sounded pretty flipping amazing! Of course I was to learn, by degrees, it doesn't quite work like that.

*   *   *

It wasn't very long before I had the opportunity to completely disregard Dad's advice on this particular point – when I secured my first job as a newspaper boy, aged 13. I did two rounds, one in the morning and one in the evening, earning the princely sum of £6.50 a week.

Now, my employer, Mr Jeffries, was a real shrewd businessman. Everyone thought he was dead shy and retiring, but I tell you, he never missed a trick, that one. Anyway, as a special favour, only for his delivery boys and girls, he had this little black book, and we could run up a tab in advance of our wages on Saturday to buy sweets, comics, footy stickers or whatever.

Well, I was in my element! My first introduction to buying

things on the never-never. I would stuff sweets like they was going out of fashion, and scrooge would carefully jot each transaction down in his little black book, watching his profits soar and my wages disappear. I remember one pay day I even owed him money, so my debt had to be carried on to the next week. I didn't care, though. In a funny way it seemed like it was all free, 'cos I never saw the money in the first place. Looking back, I suppose that's where Jeffries was so clever.

I wish I could tell you that maturing into adulthood changed my ways, but it didn't. The lure of something-for-nothing or shortcut ways to live beyond my means has never lost its attraction. I'm the credit card company's original dream customer. 'Mr Paris, as a valued customer blah blah blah, we would be delighted to extend your credit limit by a further £1,000.' I mean, how can you turn an offer like that down?

When I got my first credit cards I had the express intention of paying them off in full at the end of each month. They were purely there for convenience, I said to myself. Huh! Of course, in no time at all I was giving them the token minimum payment, convincing myself something would turn up next month so I could clear them. It wasn't just credit cards either, no! If only. Just about everything I owned was on the never-never. The new, plush, three-piece suite was no deposit, nothing to pay for a year, with interest-free credit. Well, you can't go wrong, I thought. I got my Peugeot 306 1.9 injection on some super-duper 3-2-1 special deal, with 36 low-cost monthly repayments. It all seemed so easy. The windows, cooker, washing machine, bedroom suite, shower unit . . . the whole lot, all on the never-never.

I never went that mad. Most of what I got was what you would call necessities. It's just that . . . well, I just wasn't that careful, either. In the end I didn't know which way to turn. I was in a complete state, bills and demands all over the place. Then, out of the blue, an answer to my prayers. Or so I thought.

231

* * *

It dropped through the letter box with the post one morning, all colourful and inviting: a leaflet with a picture of a grinning has-been television presenter, all teeth and no brains. 'Pay off all your debts! Car, credit cards, the lot. We clear them all within 48 hours, leaving you with just one easy payment!' Fantastic! Only now I'm paying interest on top of the interest, and the longer it goes on, the worse it gets.

The car was the first thing to go, then all the decent furniture, as you can see – and that's not to pay back what I borrowed, no. That's just to cover the mounting interest. When it gets to that state of affairs you really know you've blown it. You feel like a slave, worthless, but of course by then it's too late, much too late.

* * *

Which brings me to Julie, my wife. Moved out last week. Gone to live with her parents for a bit, temporarily like, or so she says. She can't cope any more; can't believe I didn't tell her what was happening, what a mess I'd got us into. Where she thought the money was coming from I don't know, but we didn't discuss that. She just packed a few essentials and left. Another legacy from my dad that: 'The man controls the home finances, my son. It's got nothing to do with the woman. That's the way God intended it.' (*Laughs to himself*) Soppy old duffer.

So where do I go from here? Well, who knows? *Que sera sera*, so they say. Next month, right around the corner, something might just crop up. Wait and see. You never know. You never never know. (*He smiles; lights fade to blackout.*)

Bible reference: Proverbs 22:7

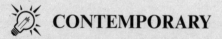 **CONTEMPORARY**

48. The Builder

'All that hard graft, and not even knowing if the foreman is gonna come back. No, no, no, I don't think so . . .'

Props

Paintbrush
Pot of paint
Overalls

BUILDER

(*Whistling and painting, he suddenly realises he is being watched by the lady of the house.*) Ooh, hello darling! Been watching me for a while, have you?

Not a bad job, is it? Even if I do say so myself. Then again, I take pride in my work, don't I! Not like the last bloke you had here! He made a terrible job. Look, bits all peeling off. No, he was a right cowboy, if you ask me. Not that I can't sort it out, like, but it just upsets me what some so-called craftsmen get away with.

Anyway, darling, I'm not one for taking too many breaks, but while I've stopped I'll tell you a funny story, right, and you will not Adam-and-Eve it – guaranteed!

* * *

I was on this job the other day, right, and I got chatting to this geezer, as you do, who said he might be able to put a nice bit of work my way. Hello, I thought – you know what I mean? I was on the old earhole straight away, 'cos you never can get enough work in my game.

Anyway, he goes on to say that he knows of this guy who's working on a humongous project – a kingdom, you might say. Well, I was all ears, weren't I? 'Cos every suss builder knows the bigger the building site, the more chance there is of copping a nice little earner. 'Yeah, mate,' he says. 'There's literally thousands of people working on this kingdom, and no one knows when or if it's gonna get finished. And the rewards – well, the rewards are massive!'

Well, by this time I was hooked, so I thought, no mucking

about, let's cut straight to the chase. So I asked him what these rewards would amount to in monetary terms and where I could find the foreman.

Now this is where it all went a bit pear-shaped! He says to me that no one has actually seen the foreman for quite some time, nor do they know when he's likely to return, and as such – wait for it – no one's been paid neither! Yeah! They just carry on willy-nilly, trusting that he will return and bring a lovely reward for them. Bunch of wombles!

Well, I hit the roof, didn't I! You're having a giraffe, I says. As if anyone in their right mind is gonna work on those pony terms. All that hard graft, and not even knowing if the foreman is gonna come back. No, no, no, I don't think so. There's no so-called faith in this trade; that's the first thing they teach you. Pay as you go, like them mobile phones, that's my motto. Let's see a bit of cash up-front, know what I mean? Now you're talking my language! None of this pansy working-for-nothing lark. I want to know where I stand, don't I? That's only professional.

Just think about it. Those absolute mullards are gonna slog their guts out all their lives on this pie-in-the-sky kingdom, rambling on about the great rewards, but what if it's all a load of tosh? They're gonna look like a right bunch of lards! No, no, you won't see me working up there. I may look a bit stupid – no comment please, sweetheart – but believe you me, I know the ways of this world.

* * *

Well, I suppose I'd better start that second coat. Won't get done just staring at it, eh! Mind you, while I've stopped, and I don't allow myself too many breaks, my old throat is as dry as a bone. I don't suppose there's any chance of a lovely cup of rosie, is there, darling? Ah, you're a diamond, you are. You are a sweetheart, no mistake, a nine-carat diamond . . .

(*Light fades to black-out.*)

Bible reference: Mark 1:15

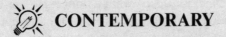 **CONTEMPORARY**

49. Survival of the Fittest

'Someone gets in your way, threatens your
territory – take 'em out. Any small sign of
weakness and baboom, it's lights out!'

GANGSTER

Do you know who got right on my wick the other day?

Go on, have a guess – no, you'll never get it. I'll tell you.
Michael Flatfeet! You know the one. Him who Irish-jigs all
over the shop like he's got a swarm of ants trapped in his
undies. Michael Flatfeet – what a ponce! He was on the telly,
right, all bouffant hair, fake tan and a hairy chest hanging
out his shiny lycra outfit. A right pillock if ever there was
one.

Now, if he came onto my manor I'd sort him out, 'cos you
see that's how it works around here. I'd say the words, click
my fingers and baboom, it's done. One serious case of Irish
jigging terminally ceased by the snapping of his stupid little
ankles.

Maybe you think that sounds excessive. Extreme and
uncalled-for ungentlemanly conduct. Well, you'd be right,
but that's the only way to get by in my line of work. Look
after number one. Survival of the fittest, that's the name of
the game.

* * *

(*Mimes looking in mirror.*) You know, I was looking in the
mirror the other day and I thought to myself, this ageing
process is a funny old business, innit! I mean, the hair stops
growing on your head, where you want it to be, right, and all
of a sudden you've got it sprouting out your nose and lug-
holes! I mean, what's all that about? What's Mother Nature
playing at? What possible use have I got for a great ugly hair
hanging out my nostril?

Still, although ageing has its disadvantages, it has its
advantages, too. You get respect, authority. You don't get to
my age in this game without buiding up a certain amount of
. . . recognition. I tell you, I've seen things that would make
the little hairs on the back of your neck all curl up. Human
life, so delicate, yet so easily disposable if and when it suits

your needs. I can order someone to be taken out, or do it myself as easy as if they were a pawn on a chessboard. What's the problem? It's survival of the fittest, innit! Someone gets in your way, threatens your territory – take 'em out. Any small sign of weakness and baboom, it's lights out.

Come on, what's up? You all watch them nature programmes on telly; what's the big difference? Look at wild animals – if one of their sprogs is a bit of a dodgy weakling, a runt, he's taken out, no questions asked. It's not personal; it's survival of the fittest. And what are we humans if not just another species of wild animal? I think we've proved that often enough.

* * *

I suppose there is a downside to my business, like with anything, I guess. You can't really have friends, anyone too close to you. Mind you, my motto's always been 'a friend in need is a pain in the rear end'. Know what I mean? If you let anyone too close, it might cause your guard to slip, cloud your otherwise crystal-clear judgement. So I don't bother with friends. I just have business colleagues, professional operatives. You know what I mean?

It's the same with women and all. I'm not one of them mugs that marries some blonde bit of stuff, just so I can flash her around, knowing all she wants is for me to get done in so she can cop all of my hard-earned. No, I'm not into all that. Boys, I'll give you a word of advice about women: women are just a load of aggro! If you give them houseroom, the next thing you know there's frilly Marks & Spencer undies draped all over the bathroom, you've got Archer's and Bacardi cluttering up your booze cabinet, and Laura Ashley floral coverings all over your quality leather furniture. You can forget all that for a start. It's a bit lonesome sometimes, on my jack, like, but it's the price you have to pay. The way the cookie crumbles. In my line of work, sacrifices have to be made. That, boys, is survival of the fittest.

Someone once told me that I was devoid of all feelings – just before I chopped him up, like. Best compliment I ever had, that, 'devoid of all feelings'. No one or nothing gets to me. That's the way I've set it up, the way it has to be.

(*He becomes uncomfortable, slightly less confident.*) Then I saw this thing on the box the other day, pictures of some foreign couple in Africa or somewhere. Four kids they had, all of them nowhere to live, not eaten for days, horrible great flies all over their faces. And they was saying on this programme that by individuals making a few cutbacks, for instance a pack of fags a week and a few drinks maybe, if we all did that, well, the problems could all be conquered. And, you know, in my position, what *I* have to say to that? I have to say – I couldn't give a monkey's. Cheers, boys, and chuck us over a light. Forget them! Don't get me wrong. I don't think it's funny seeing all that suffering. I'm not some sort of sicko that gets his jollies like that. But on the other hand I can't allow myself to be bothered about them either. They had an unlucky hand in the poker game. That's life. What can I say? In this world it's survival of the fittest. I can't allow them to have any effect on me. If I do, I'm finished.

* * *

When you look at me I'll tell you what you see: one of life's winners. I've got it all, mate. Show me a good loser, and I'll show you a loser. Know what I mean? People look at me and they want what I've got, but they'll never get it, 'cos they just play at it. They're a bit self-centred, maybe, give it a load of that, but when it comes down to it, they need to be loved. One sniff of charity and they play the philanthropist, but never make any real sacrifices. They've no real concept of what sacrifice is. I've dedicated my whole life to be what I am – number one.

240

The only problem with that is what happens when I'm not? When the cracks begin to appear – and they are. I can't let the face of that starving child touch me. That's a sign of weakness. Do you understand, comprehend? The next thing I'll want the touch of a loving wife, the security of friends. Then the cracks will open up and suck me in. I'm left weak, helpless, and if I'm not the fittest I won't survive. It's as simple as that.

But every time I close my eyes, I see him. His eyes. I'm undone by the eyes of a starving child.

Bible reference: Hebrews 9:14

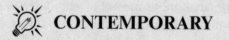 **CONTEMPORARY**

50. Don't Tell a Soul!

'She'll never live this down. Even if it's not true,
people will be saying there's no smoke
without fire!'

MARJORIE

I'm the soul of discretion, me. Everyone always says so. 'Marjorie,' they say. 'Marjorie, you are the soul of discretion.' And, to be honest, I pride myself on it. It infuriates me, all those busybodies who can't wait to get hold of a little titbit of information, or morsel of scandal, and then pass it on to all and sundry. In my opinion it displays a fatal character flaw on their part. But I don't wish to sound too judgemental! I always have a policy: if someone asks you to keep something to yourself, don't tell another soul. Or if you must, make really sure they're as reliable at being discreet as you are – you know what I mean?

For instance, *you're* all totally trustworthy, aren't you? There's no gossips among you, so if you promised not to tell another living soul I could quite safely tell you what I heard the other day, right?

* * *

I bumped into Edie – you know, the woman who serves on the tobacco counter at Safeways. We were just on the outskirts of the park. Don't know where she'd been, but I'd been to my aqua aerobics class, and she beckons me over, looking all airiated and flustered. 'Oh, Marjorie,' she says. 'I've got something to tell you.'

She put down her bags, to save her arms, at which point I knew it would be a bit of a tale. She then says, 'If I tell you this, Marj, you must promise not to tell another living soul.' Well, to be honest, I felt rather affronted!

'Edie,' I said to her. 'Edie, need you even ask?' She got my point and quickly continued.

And, in a nutshell, the thing was this. Angela Miller, oh-so-perfect Angela Miller, has gone and got herself pregnant! Well, obviously she needed a helping hand. Well, I say helping *hand* – you know what I mean. Anyway, she's only just turned 16. Now I'm sure you all know Angela, but if you don't, she was the darling of the local comprehensive. All the parents and teachers loved her and her squeaky-clean image. Two of mine were in the same year as her. Not in the same class of course – no, my two are as daft as brushes! Angela swept up an armful of A stars in her GCSEs, my Jody scraped three, in English, Science and Needlework, and my boy, Troy, only got the one, in GBH! Mind you, he is very good at it, I'll give him credit for that.

Anyway, the revelation astounded me so much that I probably wouldn't have believed it, but for Edie's source of information. She'd got the tip-off from Rosemary who works on the prescription counter at Boots. Well, that's it, I thought, it's bound to be true, 'cos if you can't trust a pharmacist in this day and age, who can you trust?

But as I said before, whatever you do, don't tell another soul, or the story will end up all twisted and exaggerated, and I wouldn't want that on my conscience.

Angela Miller. I ask you – Angela Miller! Personally, I blame the parents. I went to school with her mum, Penelope. Penny Hetherington, as she was then. Never got on with her either, always acted a couple of pegs above her station, in my opinion. Got married to a bit of a snob, too – Graham. And that's the problem, you see: people like that don't have much of a clue when it comes to raising kids. They set the bar too high, trying to be all perfect and prim and proper. And what happens? The kids rebel! You see it time and time again. Give them a bit of rope, I say – not enough to hang themselves with, but just so they have a bit of slack, if you know what I mean.

Oh, poor old Angela! She'll never live this down. Even if it's not true, people will be saying there's no smoke without fire! No, now the rumours are out it's probably best all round if it's all true.

You have to watch out for these gossips, though. I don't think they have any clue what damage they are capable of doing with a careless word or misguided comment. In all honesty, half the time they probably don't even know that they're doing it. But you didn't hear that from me, okay? Don't quote me on it. In fact, don't tell another living soul.

Bible reference: Proverbs 20:19

INDEXES

Character Index

Scripture Index

Other books by David Burt...

50 Sketches about Jesus

Picture the scene: Jesus preaching at Wembley
Stadium; a paparazzi photographer in Bethlehem;
Mary cooking spaghetti hoops on toast; the wise men
shopping in Harrods. Strange? Maybe. Funny?
Certainly. But every sketch here highlights a truth
about Jesus of Nazareth that is relevant to life today.

There's something here for all levels of expertise, and
all ages. Fully indexed by themes, occasions and Bible
references, this is an ideal resource for churches and
other groups who wish to communicate old truths in
fresh ways.

25 Sketches about Proverbs

The book of Proverbs in the Bible has long been a
source of wit and wisdom for people of various ages,
races and cultures. So what better resource could we
have for creating funny but poignant sketches about
everyday life? From subjects as diverse as betrayal,
bullying, laziness and loneliness, there is something
here for everyone! Ideal for seeker-friendly services
and all-age worship.

50 Dramatised Bible Readings

by David Burt

Reading the Bible is one of the high points in any time of worship and teaching. Yet how much effort do we give to the delivery of God's word?

Experienced actor and scriptwriter David Burt gives a practical guide to the appropriate use of dramatic techniques in reading Scripture. Each of the 50 readings which follow are given with full stage directions and tips for effective communication.

The full NIV text is provided, though the directions can easily be used in association with other translations of the Bible.

GREAT IDEAS
for Drama

50 Dramatised Bible Readings
David Burt
author of 50 Sketches about Jesus

25 Sketches about Proverbs
David Burt
Bringing Biblical proverbs to life through drama

50 Sketches about Jesus
David Burt
'A bumper bran-tub of breezy curtain-raisers'
PAUL BURBRIDGE

50 Seasonal Sketches
including weddings, baptisms, and much more
Neil Pugmire

50 Sketches for All Occasions
Compiled by Michael Botting

Helping You to Help Others